she's shameless

she's shameless

Women write about growing up, rocking out, and fighting back

Edited by Stacey May Fowles
and Megan Griffith-Greene

Tightrope Books Inc.
2009

Tightrope Books
17 Greyton Crescent
Toronto, Ontario
Canada m6e 2g1
www.tightropebooks.com

Canada Council for the Arts Conseil des Arts du Canada

ONTARIO ARTS COUNCIL
CONSEIL DES ARTS DE L'ONTARIO

editors: Stacey May Fowles and Megan Griffith-Greene
copy editors: Shirarose Wilensky and Cate Simpson
cover design: Sheila Sampath
interior section art: Sheila Sampath
typesetting: David Bigham

Produced with the support of the Canada Council for the Arts, the Ontario Arts Council and the City of Toronto through the Toronto Arts Council.

Printed in Canada

Library and Archives Canada Cataloguing in Publication

She's shameless : women write about growing up, rocking out, and fighting back / [edited by] Stacey May Fowles, Megan Griffith-Greene.

ISBN 978-0-9783351-9-9

1. Teenage girls--Canada--Biography. 2. Teenage girls--Canada--Attitudes. 3. Adolescence. I. Fowles, Stacey May II. Griffith-Greene, Megan
HQ798.S535 2009 305.235'2092271 C2009-901478-5

For all the shameless girls who know there's got to be something more,
and to all the shameless women who help them find it.

Contents

Forward: **11**

A Word From the Founders of *Shameless*

Nicole Cohen and Melinda Mattos

Introduction: **13**

This is Not an After School Special

Stacey May Fowles and Megan Griffith-Greene

Part I: **15**

Breaking the Good Girl Mould

I Don't Wear Cloaks 16
Amy Saxon Bosworth

Think Pink 19
Shannon Webb-Campbell

The Upper Hand 21
Nicole Pasulka

Girly-Girl Bites the Dust 27
Adrienne Mercer

Losing My Virginity 30
Jowita Bydlowska

We Should Make Things 35
Teri Vlassopoulos

Part II: **39**

Things They Didn't Teach Me in Health Class

Flat 40
Shannon Gerard

A Little Lesson in Lust 45
K. Bannerman

Vaginal Discharge 47
Jessica McGann

Oh, Go Eat A Hamburger 52
Shaunga Tagore

She Will Arrive 54
Karma Waltonen

Part III **57**

Getting Grounded: Run-ins with Authority

The Other Side 58
Denise Reich

Dear Monsieur Giroux 62
Dianah Smith

Red Bars 64
Catherine Graham

Split 67
Pam Park Jost

Get Well Soon 70
Maggie Dort

Part IV **75**

Relationships: For Better and Worse

Ophelia Revisited 76
Julia Serano

I'm Still Here 78
E.J. MacBain

Looking for Normal 85
Jessica Lockhart

Tethered 89
Cora Goss-Grubbs

This is Not From a Place of Perfect Memory 93
Sarah Pinder

Emma Please 96
Tara-Michelle Ziniuk

Part V **99**

Extra Credit: What I Wish I'd Known All Along

What I Learned Growing Up In Parkdale 101
Emily Pohl-Weary

Things I Wish Someone Had Told Me as a Teenaged Girl 102
Written by Zoe Whittall, illustrated by Suzy Malik

Your Mother Was The Wild One 113
Lynn Bartels

About the Contributors **115**
Acknowledgments **121**
About the Editors **122**
About *Shameless* Magazine **123**

Forward:
A Word From the Founders of Shameless
Nicole Cohen and Melinda Mattos

Sometimes anger can be a good thing, because it tells you something needs to change. *Shameless* magazine was inspired by years of frustration. We were tired of the way teen life was represented in glossy magazines as nothing more than a series of embarrassing moments and a never-ending quest for the perfect lip gloss. When we launched the magazine in 2004, we were ready to fight back.

"Welcome to *Shameless*," read our first editors' letter, "the magazine we hope will give teen media a serious kick in the ass."

Although the two of us grew up in different parts of the country, our experiences with teen magazines had been similar. We were brainy girls who loved independent music, books and politics—topics we never saw covered in *Seventeen* or *YM*. When we ended up at journalism school together and were asked to create a prototype of our dream publication, it didn't take us long to realize that we shared a common vision: a teen magazine that was fun, smart, and, most importantly, treated its readers with respect.

Most mainstream teen magazines are in the business of selling shame. They foster a climate of low self-esteem and then promise that advertisers' wares will make readers feel better about themselves. These teen magazines teach us to be ashamed of our bodies, our minds, our sexuality; ashamed if our breasts are too small or too big; if we talk too much or don't talk enough; if we don't have a boyfriend or if we would prefer to have a girlfriend. We weren't interested in selling shame. We wanted girls to be shame*less*.

Shameless started as a school project, but we quickly realized that it needed to be something more. As we finished up our assignment, we saw girls blocking off one of the busiest intersections in downtown Toronto to protest the impending war in Iraq. We heard about young women winning awards for their creativity and playing in rock bands. We met activists, artists, comedians, actors, photographers, and writers. We wanted to create a magazine that would provide space for these young women to share their stories, and we knew the magazine had to be radically different from the mainstream glossies at the grocery store check-out.

And so we created *Shameless*, with a starting budget of $0 and the help of dozens of volunteers who quickly became part of the *Shameless* community. Over the past five years, the magazine has shown why it is important for women to create their own media, and feminist media at that. *Shameless* offers a place for young and emerging Canadian writers and artists to explore ideas and issues that are important to them—issues they can't publish in other print media, from stories about genital plastic surgery (like Zoe Cormier's "Making The Cut," which was nominated for a National Magazine Award) to our back-page column on the power dynamics of everyday language.

Although publishing an independent magazine with a tiny budget and a volunteer staff is a constant challenge, *Shameless* has flourished outside the confines of corporate sponsorship. We have been free to publish articles that are feisty, controversial, and honest—the only people we are responsible to are our readers. We are pleased to see that these important conversations continue to be held daily on the magazine's blog (www.shamelessmag.com).

With the book you now hold in your hands, the current editor and publisher of *Shameless* are taking another bold step towards our original goal: giving teen media a serious kick in the ass. So put on your boots, dear reader—they can't do it without you!

Yours shamelessly,
Melinda and Nicole

Introduction:
This is Not an After School Special
Stacey May Fowles and Megan Griffith-Greene

"There are things in my life I regret, things I hope I can fix, things I still hope to accomplish, but I believe that shame is worthless. Let other people hold those scales. I have my hands full."

-Amy Saxon Bosworth, *I Don't Wear Cloaks*

This is not an after school special. The pages of this book do not contain cautionary tales about the dangers of peer pressure, how doing drugs will ruin your life, how you should save yourself until marriage, and how you should stay in school.

In fact, it's always really bothered us the way that people talk about, and to, youth. Most don't give young people all that much credit—after all, teens are too young to make their own decisions; they are apathetic and shallow, reckless and thoughtless, right? That popular caricature is stupid, offensive, and, more often than not, hypocritical.

So—since we've always been the kind of people to make our own fun—we wanted to create an anthology to bust that condescension, where women told the truth about their lives as teenagers, bullshit and rhetoric free. What we received from our call for submissions was pretty inspiring. We got honest stories from women about having sex and falling in love, standing up to parents and teachers, coming out, making choices about their bodies, and defining identity in opposition to distorted expectations. The writers are brave, strong, and pissed off. They refuse to be silent. They refuse to be good girls. They refuse to be ashamed.

They are the teenagers we knew and the teenagers we were.

We've been celebrating this attitude in the pages of *Shameless* magazine for more than five years: honest, accessible, and meaningful writing for teen girls overlooked by the mainstream. We don't patronize or preach, and we know there's more to life than makeup tips. Young women deserve to be heard; their experiences are powerful and they're not alone in feeling frustrated with the status quo.

We hope that the personal stories in this book inspire and empower you in the same way they did us. More importantly, we hope that in a world that constantly pushes girls to be something they're not, you'll see your experiences and yourself reflected in these pages.

No bullshit. No caricatures. No shame.

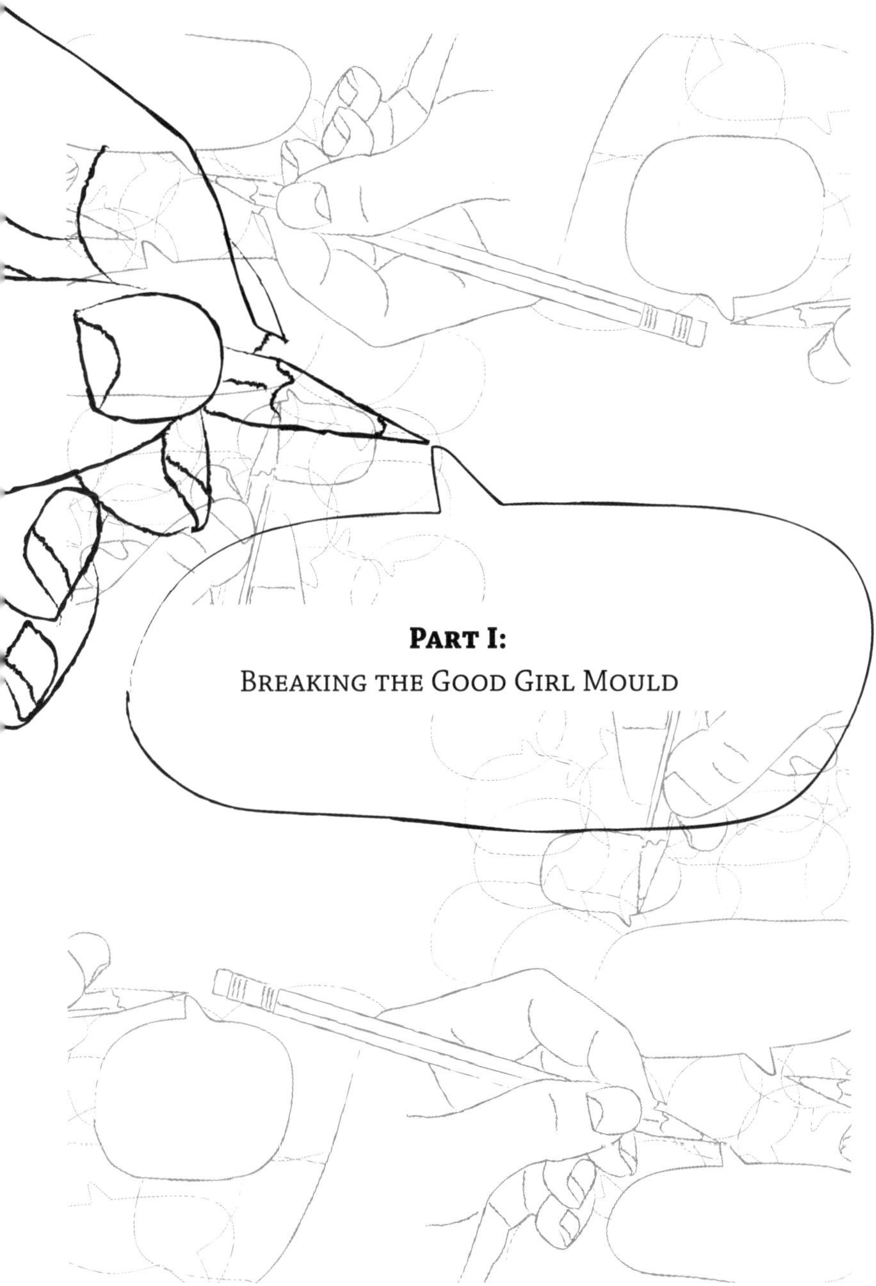

Part I:
Breaking the Good Girl Mould

I Don't Wear Cloaks

Amy Saxon Bosworth

When I was small, an older cousin coaxed me into sprinkling salt onto a slug in our grandfather's English ivy garden. I watched with shame as the creature suffered and died. I remembered this as I sat against the gray cinder block wall on the cold gym floor of my high school one day after winter break. I could think of only the slug curled in my belly. I was sixteen years old.

I had made an appointment to have the little slug salted but changed my mind after a I saw a tiny tot at the rodeo, dressed in Wranglers and boots, wearing a starched white shirt. The tiny cowboy looked so precarious perched so high on his father's shoulders, so fragile, so human. I tried to reconcile that with what moved within me. I made up my mind: the little slug would grow.

At sixteen, I was pretty, popular, and on the fast track; headed on a full scholarship to the state's best college. I was a member of the National Honor Society, on the debate team and a star of the Academic Decathlon. Home was a different story: things were thrown and broken; hair was pulled; words were hurled; fingernails gouged flesh. I found solace in a nice middle-class boy and dreamed about getting the hell out.

That winter, I starred in a theatrical production *The Diary of Anne Frank*. Every night I climbed upon that stage, playing a young girl who was trapped and persecuted. I was sixteen weeks along. When I felt the first movement, I thought I could feel the baby unfurl from its trappings. I imagined its little appendages poking at me from within, insect-like. The tears on stage that night were real.

My co-star Peter helped me bind my breasts with tape and bandages. Peter had just come out of the closet; a good friend, he was the first to guess. He kissed me tenderly each night under the stage lights as the weeks wore on. I told him that if I had a girl I would name her Anneliese; if it was a boy I would call him Blake, after a friend who died of leukemia. I wanted my child to have a strong soul.

I was not anxious to spill the pee on the stick to my parents. My father, a lifetime law enforcement man, had—in uniform—sternly confronted one boy who dared to date me without permission. There was talk of daddy running for Justice of the Peace that spring, and a pregnant daughter doesn't make for a good campaign platform in the heart of the Bible Belt. And my mother was the cruel one. So I swallowed my tears and used a ponytail holder to fasten my blue jeans. I jotted a life plan in a pink spiral notebook, stalling for time. I knew the longer I waited the less control they had, the more power I gained.

When the time came, I pretended I was Valerie Bertinelli in a movie of the week. I left a note on my pillow and drove away, but my plan backfired when my parents didn't check my bedroom. Long past curfew, impatient, I called and dumped the news on them.

Tears that my mother never wasted on me before now flowed at the disgrace I had brought her. Three days later I was in full blooming maternity outfits: everything back then had huge blossoming flowers. Three weeks later I was married to my high school sweetheart on his eighteenth birthday. Three months later I was sitting in my very own home nursing my newborn while doing calculus homework.

When my school found out, they counseled me on ways to "go away." They told me that *of course things like this happen to girls like you but they are taken care of early*. One teacher refused to give me an A because I was a poor role model. My National Honor Society candle was snuffed out; I was not invited back. My honors graduation tassels were inexplicably "lost." Today, I do not receive invitations to class reunions.

But my son—who's a foot taller than me now—is the most honorable thing I have ever achieved. There are things in my life I regret, things I hope I can fix, things I still hope to accomplish, but I believe that shame is worthless. Let other people hold those scales. I have my hands full.

When I see a young girl ripe with life, I smile. I don't narrow my eyebrows in judgment. I breathe and I remember. I remember standing on stage in a spotlight, wishing for the freedom of a life without condemnation. I meet her eyes with tears of joy and I whisper to her, "Peace."

"Shame is pride's cloak."—William Blake

Think Pink

Shannon Webb-Campbell

On an unexpected June afternoon, in Calgary, Alberta, Diane gave birth to 3.5 pound me—two months premature. For a few long hours I was tagged Tiffany, but my father quickly changed his mind and opted for Shannon: a traditional Irish name. Being a Newfoundlander, he wanted to draw on the sturdiness of his roots. He named his daughter after a rushing river instead of some Audrey Hepburn jewelry store. I fit in the neighbourhood, too: the young boys next door were named Shane and Shamus.

But the river quickly quieted to a trickle. My mother decked me out in pale pink doll's clothing (I was too small to fit regular-sized newborn attire.) I was going to be her little girl—a doll-sized bundle of salivating joy. (In truth, I looked more like my dad.)

Slowly I made baby steps into a monochromatic childhood, dressed head-to-toe in pink and white outfits. From the floors of my bedroom to the crib where I slept, everything was pink: pink balloons, pink blankets, pink teddy bears, pink flowers, pink diapers, pink facecloths, pink baby wipes.

Pink.

I grew a little older, stuck in a cotton-candy-coloured cloud. When other girls were playing soccer, jumping rope, or climbing in trees, I was glued to glossy magazines that taught me how to count calories. I indulged in small pink packets of artificial sweetener, one-calorie cream soda and sugar-free strawberry candies.

As a teenager, I tried everything to be girly. Hairbrush, comb, curling iron, blow dryer, crimper, hair pick, elastics, hairspray, gel, clips, and cosmetics were all a single hue.

Every night I spent an hour in front of the VCR trying to get Buns of Steel and shape my body like Cindy Crawford, in her fuchsia spandex leotard. One night huffing and puffing through my lunges and crunches, I felt a wave of euphoria that made me tingle and blush. I lay there on my back on the pink-carpeted floor of my mother's living room, wet with sweat, breathing heavily. I wasn't quite sure what it was at first, but it started from a secret pink place.

Over the next few years I got in touch with this pink, fleshy part of myself, under the sheets, late at night when mom was asleep.

I traded in the glossy how-to-guides for magazines like *Bitch* and *Bust*. I no longer felt that things divided into pink or blue. My wardrobe turned black.

Late one night I found myself alone at a nearby watering hole, dressed to kill in black: boots, dress, and overcoat, twinkling guitar, and spoken word winding through the space. Next to me on the barstool sat a girl with pink hair drinking a vodka and cranberry.

I smiled. She smiled back.

Suddenly the world seemed pink in a new way. I found pink again: this time shaped like an inverted triangle that represents gay pride.

Not only am I a woman, I'm a pink woman. I'm a pink woman who loves the pink of other women.

The Upper Hand

Nicole Pasulka

Leah must have felt like a peacock slumming it with a pigeon. She drove a Mercedes convertible, lived in a house with a basketball court and spent, for a high school student, what seemed like an impossible amount of time on vacation in Mexico. I, on the other hand, listened to Cypress Hill on repeat, had seven holes in my right ear, two in my left, and enjoyed a stubborn, almost irrational, hatred of bras.

In 1997, grungy kids were massively suspicious of preppy girls who wore flared jeans and shoes with heels instead of work jackets and flannel shirts from dad's closet. But Leah, though neat and clean, wasn't just some vapid rich girl. She made frequent (if vague) mentions of running away, alcohol poisoning, and car accidents. She had privilege, but she also had secrets. And so, during the summer between grades nine and ten, despite our superficial differences, I could usually be found in Leah's car going for fast food, smoking clove cigarettes, and talking about boys and sex.

Though she was two years older than me, Leah was still a virgin. In a friendship where she provided the transportation, the social status, and sometimes even the money, I was happy to have the upper hand by being casually authoritative about all things sexual.

"Oh, of course it will hurt a bit the first time," I told her as we sprawled on matching white sofas in her TV room. "Just tough it out, eventually it will feel good."

My single attempt at sex to that point had ended with a broken condom and a week of sleepless nights until my next period, but I'd repeat anything I heard or read that sounded insightful or accurate. Plus I had had sex. That, at least, was true.

Through Leah's job at the movie theatre, I met an eighteen-year-old metalhead named Alex, one of the nicest guys I've ever known. Alex and Leah would sneak me into matinees, or out to smoke by the dumpster behind the theatre. When Alex and I first starting going out, Leah was around a lot, and even though she'd introduced us, it sometimes felt like she thought Alex was out of my league.

"Alex is so sweet and so great. He's really into you. Don't screw it up and break his heart," she warned me.

Leah could have easily dated Alex, if she'd wanted to. Instead, her boyfriend was a stocky lacrosse player named Brendan with a T-top car and a slight lisp. Brendan treated me with the bored forbearance he might show a younger sister or cousin. I repaid the favour by pretending he didn't exist.

After dating about a month, Alex and I started sleeping together—well, sleeping together isn't quite accurate. We'd have sex in the car; on the floor; in the shower; once we even did it in the shed at his parents' house. The sex wasn't disastrous, particularly intense, or even romantic; it was mostly just fun and frequent. Considering the integral role she'd played in bringing us together, I naturally kept Leah updated on all the gory details.

"Yesterday Alex and I were having sex in his parents' room and they almost walked in on us."

"Mm-hm," Leah replied distractedly as she pulled clothes out of her closet for me to try on.

"Don't you think it's gross to have sex in the room where his parents sleep?" This was more of a judgment than an actual question. It brought the conversation to an immediate halt.

All of the sudden, Leah wasn't interested in hearing about or analyzing my sex life. I assumed that she was jealous, or at least didn't like being reminded of what was missing from her relationship with Brendan. And so I ignored her disinterest and kept dishing the dirt.

One night, at the end of the summer, I went with Leah and Brendan to a party at another lacrosse player's house. Boys I'd seen in the halls at school, but never spoken to, lined up to funnel beers in the kitchen. Leah, though she threw back mixed drinks and chatted comfortably, was at the party because she was Brendan's girlfriend. I had even less reason to be there. When Leah and Brendan disappeared upstairs, some of his friends tried to convince me to do shots with them, acting as though they were trying to get a family pet drunk. I had yet to discover the social benefits of alcohol at awkward parties, and didn't want to provide entertainment for a bunch of jocks, so I stayed sober, watching others down can after can of cheap beer.

After I'd endured about a half-hour of relentless coaxing from two eleventh graders in warm-up suits, Leah stumbled downstairs and made a beeline toward me.

"Brendan just went down on me," she slurred in my ear.

"Wow." I looked around making sure no guys with lacrosse sticks were in earshot.

Suddenly, her hands were on my face, blocking the view of our mouths. She kissed me, hard. To anyone across the room, it must have looked like she was telling a secret. I guess she sort of was.

I'd always wanted to kiss a girl. I considered myself open-minded and adventurous, but it was more than that. Sometimes, in the locker room after gym class, I caught myself staring when Jen Sheckly changed out of her swimsuit. Underneath stacks of old books in my closet were *Playboys* my friend Kirsten and I had stolen from her stepfather. We laughed about how perverted and disgusting he was for having them, but it wasn't long before I learned every name, age, and favourite pastime of the pinups. Even though I had a boyfriend and didn't feel like a lesbian, I imagined what it would be like to have a girl close to me and know for sure that she wanted me to kiss her.

Leah was sleeping at my house that night. My parents were still out when Brendan dropped us off. She fell twice on the way up my front steps, and had to lean on my shoulder as we climbed the stairs to my room.

Sitting together on the bed, Leah put her arm around my waist.

"Did you like what I did before, at the party?"

I nodded, afraid I'd say the wrong thing and lose the chance to kiss her again, still worried that the come-ons were a trap.

"Do you want to do it again?"

Another nod, and we did.

As she kissed me, Leah asked if I thought she was pretty. Her mouth muffled my enthusiastic, "Yes!"

Clothes started to come off.

If you had asked which of my female friends might have slept with me,

Leah would never have made the list. But, that night, when I had sex with Leah, we knew exactly what to do.

The next day, we had a secret. We'd slept late and didn't talk much, but I couldn't believe how close to her I felt. After breakfast, my mom drove Leah home. I was elated. She and I could do this whenever we wanted to. It felt like someone had unlocked a safe full of sexy diamonds and told me to take whatever I could carry.

At her house later that day, we hung out in the pool. After showering, I walked topless from the bathroom into her bedroom.

Leah looked me up and down indifferently, "Oh, you know, I used to think you had big boobs, but now I see that you're just really skinny—your boobs actually aren't any bigger than mine."

I laughed and pulled on the bottom of her shirt suggestively.

"Uh. Yeah. We're not doing that anymore." She took a step backwards. "I mean—it's not going to happen again."

I don't know if my face visibly fell, but my hopes sure crashed to the ground. It was stupid to have thought things could be any different than Leah being with Brendan, and me with Alex.

I told Alex what happened with Leah, making it clear it was "no big deal and not that great." He was too sweet and maybe too insecure to be angry. Plus fooling around with a girl wasn't cheating, he reasoned; it was just hot and kind of freaky.

By the time Alex and I broke up almost two years later, I hadn't spoken to Leah for over a year. I had a new group of friends, a buzz cut, and a nose ring. Despite sporting an androgynous look, that night had become an aberration in my otherwise totally straight existence. I'd tried that "bisexual" thing, and it just didn't work out. Guys were for me; girls were too much trouble.

I was so sure of my heterosexuality, I'd ridicule anyone who challenged it. Helga, a butch, red-haired foreign exchange student who cruised me in the halls in grade eleven was met with harsh, unforgiving glares.

"Why do these lesbians always try to pick me up?!" I'd complain to my straight, usually male, companions. "Just because I have a buzz cut and wear men's clothing, they assume I'm gay. It's so insulting." My friends just laughed, elbowing me any time Helga shot amorous glances during a passing period.

Once, on a school trip, a girl from another high school had her friend approach me while I was having lunch with my own classmates.

"My friend, um, thinks you're cute. My friend wants to know if you'll let me take your picture." She hadn't mentioned that her "friend" was a girl, but I'd noticed them pointing and whispering.

"I think it's ridiculous your friend can't just come up and talk to me, if your friend wants to know me so badly. What is your friend so afraid of?" Considering my reaction, her fears were justified. Weird as it is to ask to photograph a stranger, it certainly didn't warrant ridiculing an understandably gun-shy girl.

In college I came across more lesbians and had more opportunities to complain about their unwanted attention. In my first year, I completely ignored Christina, a lanky, stylish girl that I'd even admitted was attractive. Instead, I favoured a series of scruffy, indifferent boys whose dorm rooms boasted fridges of beer and candy dishes of condoms.

In retrospect, all this hostility made it clear: I wasn't fighting off women, I was fighting off my attraction to them. I dismissed girls the way Leah had dismissed me, and I convinced myself that because I enjoyed sex and relationships with men, there was no way I could or would date a woman. Plus, what self-respecting lesbian would accept me once I admitted finding a chest covered in hair as attractive as one bursting out of a bra?

There was no moment of clarity, but after college my curiosity, my desire, and the memory of my night with Leah got the best of me. I grew up, my defenses broke down, and I started to pursue women.

On a plane back from visiting my parents one Christmas, I was seated next to a girl named Kaitlin. She greeted me with a shy, crooked smile, her shaggy brown hair peeking out from a newsboy hat. During the flight, her knee periodically brushed against mine. When this happened, my entire brain and body would focus on the single point of contact until it seemed to be vibrating.

The plane landed in New York City and she asked if I wanted to share a cab back to Brooklyn, where we both had apartments. The car dropped us off between our houses, and as we walked down the street oversized picture-perfect snowflakes stuck to our coats and luggage.

Kaitlin was throwing a party at a lesbian bar later that month. She gave me a flyer before we parted ways. But, by the time the party rolled around, we were already spending most nights together.

For years I'd been waiting to be able to kiss a girl—every day, whenever I wanted—who also wanted to kiss me. Dating a girl was not the drama-fest that, in my fear and ignorance, I had assumed it would be. It was warm, and close, and comfortable. And, since both Kaitlin and I, at some point in the past, had trouble admitting our feelings for women, it felt like we were members of a club unknown to people who didn't understand or had never considered the real power and beauty of same-sex attraction.

Kaitlin and I weren't together forever, but I still have a photo of us kissing at a party in a crowd of people. Her arms are wrapped around my waist, our faces pressed together, with no secrets in sight.

Girly-Girl Bites the Dust

Adrienne Mercer

At thirty-seven years old and counting, I am happy as hell to have failed as a girly-girl.

I own no dressy shoes. I skip expensive lipsticks in favour of ChapStick. I have been known to go to work with red grill marks on my neck after trying to operate a hairdryer and drink a cup of coffee at the same time. I move through my adult life accepting that I'll never be one of those effortlessly glamorous, windswept women featured (and airbrushed) in magazines. Every now and then I say a quiet Hallelujah for that.

It's not that I didn't want to be girly. I tried *hard*. From grade nine through grade twelve I spent hours every week poring over teen magazines. *Makeup How-Tos, Beauty Dos and Don'ts, Helpful Hair Hints*—none of it escaped my scrutiny. I was well read in the classics, but I still preferred to study how to achieve 100 different hairstyles with the aid of a round brush and a few bobby pins. I wanted it all—sun-kissed beauty, flawless skin, and, of course, that special boy—but *Sweet Valley High* was not my destiny.

I grew up with rheumatoid arthritis, a chronic illness I was diagnosed with when I was three years old. Arthritis turned everyday things like getting out of bed, opening a carton of milk, walking to school, carrying textbooks—or magazines—into frustrating, painful battles. By the age of sixteen I had ingested a barrage of anti-inflammatory medications, allowed a specialist to inject steroids directly into my knee joints, and recovered from two arthroscopic surgeries. Obviously, the beauty articles I was reading at the time were superficial by comparison, but I wanted to fit in. I spent hours in the bathroom with a magazine open beside the sink, studying an enlarged photograph of an overly pink cheekbone, hoping that the step-by-step makeup application instructions would help me look and feel as carefree as the model in the magazine.

Morning routine circa 1987:

1. Wake up. Take arthritis medication.
2. Shower or bathe in invigorating scented product of the month.
3. While wrapped in towel, apply moisturizer, concealer, foundation, pressed or loose powder or combination, eye shadow in three coordinating shades, eyeliner, mascara (two coats), lip liner, lipstick (use a brush!), lip gloss. Blot.
4. Dry hair using several different brushes.
5. Curl hair with a barrel iron. Tease bangs just so. Ignore aching in shoulders, elbows, and wrists.
6. Apply 14-hour aerosol hairspray of choice. (What ozone layer?)
7. Ignore pre-teen brother banging on the bathroom door. Eventually emerge when a frustrated parent finally demands it.
8. Assess closet. Pull on tapered jeans and shaker-knit sweater, or some variation of same.
9. Re-tease bangs.
10. Quickly eat breakfast.
11. Reapply lip liner, lipstick, lip gloss. Blot. Worry that lipstick is the wrong shade or intensity.
12. Cram all makeup, at least one brush, and 14-hour aerosol hairspray canister into large purse. Clip on Walkman (without flattening hair).
13. Pack much smaller bag with schoolwork and lunch. Spritz on perfume.
14. Step into orthopedic shoes. (Self-esteem plummets.)
15. Meet girlfriends for walk to school. Arrive feeling slightly nauseous due to co-mingling of various perfumes and hairsprays. Walk immediately to girls' washroom and repeat entire makeup routine in preparation for first class.

To my friends and acquaintances I am sure that I fit in just fine, but I never felt like part of things. In my orthopedic shoes and working splint (so my wrist and fingers would not ache from hours of writing) I felt like an imposter in the world of Teen Beauty. Look pretty and flirt with boys? Some days my feet and ankles were so sore that I could barely make it to class. My problems had little to do with arthritis, of course, and even less to do with my perceived lack of fashion and beauty know-how. My problem was self-doubt. Somehow I failed to see that none of my friends looked like magazine models—and I didn't spend hours mercilessly picking their looks apart. Somehow I couldn't grasp that those windswept "beauties" I envied were styled to sell the clothes and beauty and hair-care products that the magazines advertised. Magazines were *supposed* to make me feel bad about myself. They were *supposed* to make me want products I didn't need and a glamorous life that didn't exist—for me or for anyone else.

Somehow, I fell for all of it.

Looking back, I am glad for the insecurity I felt, and for my supposed failure at girly-girldom. Had I been a confident, sun-kissed teen embedded in a specific aesthetic, I might never have discovered the true loves I found in my twenties: alternative journalism, community radio, indie bands, and thrifting. I may not have moved from Victoria, BC to Ottawa, ON for a co-op journalism placement, or later relocated to a rural B.C. village of 1700 people for my first job as a newspaper editor.

Had I been a successful girly-girl, I might now have a different career, a different partner, a different situation entirely. I might have done great things—but I wouldn't truly be me. I'll take the life I've got—ChapStick, hairdryer mishaps, and all.

Losing My Virginity

Jowita Bydlowska

Her clean strong voice burst out like a dozen birds from one of the windows of the attic above the stables.

"Sta-an do-on't you lea-ave me, why won't you come ba-ack?"

The German tourists looked up, searching for the sound. The song continued. The woman loved Stan. Stan had left the woman. The woman realized that life wasn't worth living. When it was over, the Germans clapped and shouted enthusiastically. "Wie schön! Bravo! Bravo! Bis! Bis!"

I knew she was only singing to impress Valdek. It wouldn't work: he once said he was tone-deaf and colour-blind. Besides, I was the one he had asked to sit on his lap the night before. He played with *my* hair. He said he *loved* my hair.

The smiling German tourists demanded to know when the next performance would be starting. "Fuck. Nein, nein," I scraped my pitchfork against the asphalt, "Nein. No more. Hotel!" I pointed toward it. We stood facing each other, blinking in the hot, hot sun. Eventually the Germans trotted away.

It was my last day at the stables. It was my last day being a virgin. But I didn't know that yet.

The stables were a part of a luxury hotel complex in Mikolajki, Poland, favoured by middle-aged German couples and by Russian men with their young, beautiful, bored female companions.

Anna and I were almost fifteen. We were there with Anna's dad, Michal, a New Age kind of dude who would take off his Speedo when suntanning. He told us that he liked French women best because they're so uninhibited.

Michal said we were free to do whatever, as long as we didn't do anything stupid. I couldn't imagine what that stupid thing could be, since we were allowed to drink Piña Coladas and hang out in the adult disco, where topless dancers whirled around poles in front of neon signs that flashed the word FUN. If booze and peelers were okay, then I figured that "stupid" would have to involve a gun, a harvested human kidney and a brick of heroin.

We spent the days suntanning and working at the stables: shoveling horse crap and riding horses. We ate greasy French fries and talked about Anna's chances of becoming the next Mariah Carey. We talked about Anna's secret plan. She was going to lose her virginity this summer.

We had just read in a magazine about Kate Moss and how she lamented being the last in her class to lose her virginity. She was fourteen when she did it. We didn't particularly look up to Kate Moss, but she seemed to have the world's attention. So Anna decided we had to lose our virginity too that summer. Otherwise, we would die old, unwanted, surrounded by cats and regret.

I wasn't convinced. I hadn't even been kissed yet. Okay, I had read *The Story of O*. But I had also just seen Disney's *The Little Mermaid*. I bought my first grown-up black dress. But I also bought myself a crushed-velvet bear in the hotel. I was still confused.

Anna didn't seem to be. Anna wore makeup. She owned a bottle of perfume called Fiji and read her mother's *In Style* magazine. Anna talked about penises. She told me I should be masturbating. She was masturbating; it was not a big deal. She owned a box of condoms.

Anna also sought information from an older girl, Kasia, who trained at the stables. Kasia said that once a non-virgin, Anna would officially be a woman. People would know. She would be noticed more. Men would pay her compliments, follow her home, demand her phone number, send flowers. Anna and Kasia went for long walks, whispering and giggling. Theirs was an exclusive club: the virginity extermination club.

Me? I show-jumped. I was uncoordinated and afraid of horses: their massive necks and thunder-strong legs. I wanted to ride so bad so I shoved the fear down my throat. After lots of practice, I started to get better, more confident. I started to sit tighter in the saddle. I had a great teacher. His name was Valdek and he was old. He was so old I called him "Sir".

He was at least thirty-two. He had a wife, and a child who had a lolling, sleepy head that was too big, like there was something wrong with it.

There were other men at the stables. There was Matthew who was popular with the bored Russian girlfriends. There was Rafael, Valdek's brother, who was in love with the daughter of the helicopter pilot. There was Tom who had just got married and just had a baby. There was Anna's father, Michal.

The days continued, warm and sunny; the lake by the hotel was blue and clear, reflecting the bees and the helicopter, which buzzed lazily above our heads. At the stables, we worked hard but laughed a lot. It was all worry-free most of the time.

One day, Anna and I sat in the sauna by the pool.

"I think I picked him," Anna said.

"Picked who?"

"Him. My deflowerer."

"Your what?"

"My deflowerer," said Anna, "The person who is going to deflower me? The man I am going to lose my virginity to?"

"Deflowerer is not even a word."

"Whatever. Anyway. I picked him."

"Who is it?"

"Wouldn't you like to know."

"No," I said.

But it made her mission more plausible, she was going to become a woman. She was going to be different from me, a grown-up: a person who has sex. It meant that we would not be able to do our stupid girl things, like dressing up in her slutty mother's clothes when her mother was out, pretending to be famous or on drugs. Instead, she would wear the slutty clothes for real, and become famous and do drugs. I didn't know if sex did that to you for sure, but it seemed that way. Just look at Kate Moss.

"It's Valdek."

"You're an idiot," I said and she got up, cracked open the hot sauna door and stopped speaking to me.

I knew that Anna had been following Valdek, asking him hundreds of questions, telling him about her future as an opera singer. I thought she was just being a teacher's pet; I never thought that she could actually *like*-like him.

For the next two days Anna avoided me and spent time with Kasia. I worked and rode horses until I was sweating under my breasts. I was bitter, jealous of their friendship and their secrets.

I couldn't tell if Valdek was good-looking: he was too old to tell. Sometimes he wore hideous two-toned track suits because he couldn't recognize colour. He was brusque with me and yelled at me for not riding properly.

But I started listening closer. "You have good hips," he'd say, as he watched me. I felt enchanted, thrilled and disgusted at the same time.

One night, we all went to the adult disco. When there were no dancers, the guys would pay more attention to us. Michal half-heartedly told us not to drink too much. We got tipsy and danced on the dance floor in front of the stage, made out of mirror tiles.

Anna whispered in my ear about how incredibly sexy Valdek was, how manly. She was being my best friend again. Kasia was away. We watched Valdek dance. He danced like a monkey, I thought, but after a few drinks, his monkey moves became more like animal magnetism.

For the first time, I heard a note of desperation in his voice, in the way he joked with us. Matthew said I was sexy. A quiet explosion that slid down my legs. Sexy. I didn't giggle. I said, "Yeah, I know."

The men laughed. Anna fell quiet. She strained to joke but was losing to my newfound power. The more drinks, the more obvious the message: men wanted something. And I could navigate it better than Anna. I discovered that I could flirt. Valdek said he loved how pretty and long my hair was. He buried his nose in my hair. I felt shivers. No one had ever done anything that intimate to me before.

In the bathroom, I told Anna that I too wanted to lose my virginity. I wanted more of that attention; I wanted to become a woman.

I drank more Piña Coladas, Blue Lagoons, and Green Apples, and ended up on Valdek's lap. I couldn't see Anna anywhere. I couldn't see, period.

The next day, Anna sang her mournful, beautiful song. It was one of those songs her voice teacher told her to practise with because it was full of difficult scales. It was a song about lost love. Anna sang it for Valdek. Anna sang it for me. She sang it right from her heart. We broke her heart.

That afternoon, I rode one of the prize horses, the six-foot brown Hanoverian with muscles like liquid moving underneath its skin. I straightened out in the saddle, thrust my tiny breasts out.

My hair felt full of sun; it was wild and bouncing off my back. I arched my back.

When I got off the horse, Anna said, "I saw what you were doing."

"I wasn't doing anything."

"I can't believe it." Anna said and her voice was dark.

I watched her disappear in Kasia's red little car. She flipped me the finger when I waved for them to stop.

In the evening, I ran after Valdek as he was leaving the stables. I thought about his wife and the big-headed baby for a moment and then I pushed it away. This wasn't about him anyway. He grabbed my face in his huge hands and kissed me wetly when I told him what I wanted to do. That was my first kiss.

He rented a room in the luxury hotel. We went downstairs to drink vodka and didn't speak much. Valdek put his hand on my thigh. It sat there, heavy and big. I thought about his horrible purple silk shirt, how he probably wore it to mark the occasion. How pathetic. I thought how I wouldn't be able to share any of this with my best friend, Anna. Anna and I were kaput. Lucky me, I had men.

We watched the dancers. The club was black and blue with neon signs: FUN, FUN, FUN. The dancers moved in and out of the darkness. Under the strobe lights, their skin would burst with light from stick-on faux diamonds. The men at other tables stared hypnotized. I had on a big, green sweater that I had bought in an army store and that made me look shapeless. Underneath, I wore my black grown-up dress.

The next morning, I sneaked out of the hotel room before Valdek woke up. I thought it would hurt him to wake up alone. I would have one up on him.

I watched Madonna's new video "Rain" in the hotel lobby. I decided not to go back to the stables to get my stuff. I felt thrilled about what had happened, but I was too embarrassed to face Anna.

I went straight to the train station and got a ticket home. I looked around to see if people were looking at me differently. No one was looking at me. I watched my reflection in the glass door. Same.

Back in my hometown, I walked home. A car driving by erupted in catcalls and whistles. I walked straight into a hair salon and got my hair cut off.

WE SHOULD MAKE THINGS

Teri Vlassopoulos

There was a time when I wore the same pair of pants every day. They were navy blue and corduroy and they fit perfectly. The bum disintegrated from too many days of sitting on uncomfortable school chairs or cross-legged on asphalt and cement curbs. When the material thinned out to an obscene level, I patched it up with bits of fabric, stabbing my fingers while teaching myself how to sew. I was sixteen and then I was seventeen, and I wore those pants and for a while I got really quiet.

The quiet of adolescence doesn't feel like quiet at the time. I have pages of journals filled with my tight handwriting—all rounded letters, ellipses, and question marks. I stayed up late. I wrote. I had so many words, but I wasn't sure who I could trust them with, so I swallowed them up instead. The quiet worried my parents, and it worried my friends, and even teachers would look at me quizzically, probably used to these kinds of muted theatrics, but still curious about my vow of silence.

The root of it was a deep sense of restlessness. I was looking for something, but I just wasn't sure what it was, and there was only so far I could walk, only so far I could take the subway to pursue the search. So, I did what I could. I developed obsessions. Mostly with bands, reading song lyrics like tea leaves and hoping to catch a glimpse of my future.

Other obsessions were more obscure, like that month-long period I was really into making soup, soothed by the repetitive but satisfying task of chopping vegetables into tiny, perfect cubes. I tried to grow my hair really, really long. I tried knitting. But I was still restless.

Discovering zines seems like a fluky accident. I read about a Sloan fanzine in the pages of *Exclaim!* magazine and, on a whim, mailed some stamps and loose change to a girl in Ontario. I wasn't exactly sure what I'd receive in return. When I found a little homemade, photocopied booklet in the mailbox, I was surprised, but also relieved. Maybe this was the kind of thing I had been looking for. It felt illicit and inspiring, the way first kisses make you gasp. I liked the zine but, even more, I liked the concept of zines. I started ordering more of them, blindly sending letters and quarters to girls and boys all over Canada and the United States.

This is how you make a zine: get some paper, a good, dark pen, a pair of scissors, and a glue stick. A computer or typewriter will help, but they're not requirements. Find some pictures, ones with high contrast. Draw something. Make pretty borders. Or don't do any of this stuff. Once you have the words, the layout is up to you. Mostly, just write.

My first zine was four pages, back and front, typed out on thin white paper, full of non-sequitur musings about Eric's Trip and snowstorms. I photocopied it at a corner shop down the street, annoying the clerk with my multiple questions about double-sided copies, and then I sewed each copy together by hand, the same way I had patched my favourite pants. I took a deep breath and mailed them out.

The truth is that it's hard for me to stomach my old zines, especially the early ones. They were so uncertain. I reread them now and remember how tentative I felt about the state of my life. It's like I wrote in a kind of code, not wanting to reveal too much, but simultaneously wanting to spill my guts. I wrote about changes in the weather: snowy winters; hot, hot summers. As I got bolder I revealed more, told longer stories, named names. Most of it I would never commit to paper and distribute publicly today, but that's because I don't have to be heard the way I needed to be heard when I was seventeen.

I wrote awkwardly structured sentences like:

I've been walking a lot lately. When the new year came I had a notion that perhaps winter was going to end early, that maybe for one year it would end before I ever had the chance to really become tired of it. But, of course, that is not the case, and last Thursday morning the snowfall began again as I was sitting in the brownish classroom which was mine when I was in grade 11, writing my calculus exam.

And I made things that looked like:

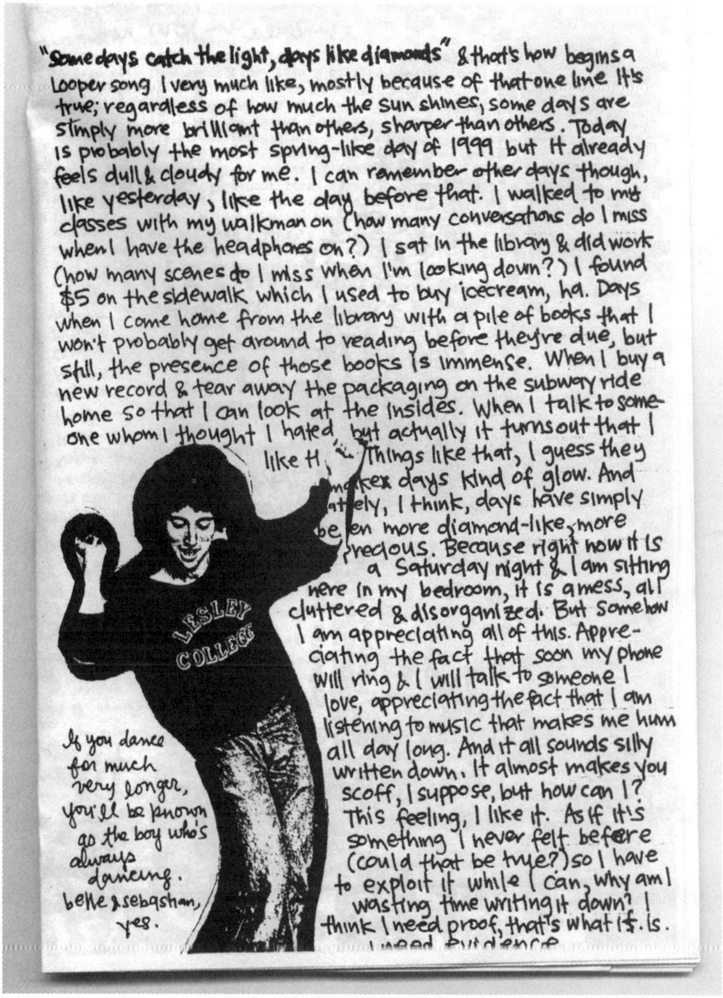
"Somedays catch the light, days like diamonds" & that's how begins a
Looper song I very much like, mostly because of that one line. It's
true; regardless of how much the sun shines, some days are
simply more brilliant than others, sharper than others. Today
is probably the most spring-like day of 1999 but it already
feels dull & cloudy for me. I can remember other days though,
like yesterday, like the day before that. I walked to my
classes with my walkman on (how many conversations do I miss
when I have the headphones on?) I sat in the library & did work
(how many scenes do I miss when I'm looking down?) I found
$5 on the sidewalk which I used to buy icecream, ha. Days
when I come home from the library with a pile of books that I
won't probably get around to reading before they're due, but
still, the presence of those books is immense. When I buy a
new record & tear away the packaging on the subway ride
home so that I can look at the insides. When I talk to some-
one whom I thought I hated but actually it turns out that I
like it. Things like that, I guess they
make days kind of glow. And
lately, I think, days have simply
been more diamond-like, more
precious. Because right now it is
a Saturday night & I am sitting
here in my bedroom, it is a mess, all
cluttered & disorganized. But somehow
I am appreciating all of this. Appre-
ciating the fact that soon my phone
will ring & I will talk to someone I
love, appreciating the fact that I am
listening to music that makes me hum
all day long. And it all sounds silly
written down. It almost makes you
scoff, I suppose, but how can I?
This feeling, I like it. As if it's
something I never felt before
(could that be true?) so I have
to exploit it while I can, why am I
wasting time writing it down? I
think I need proof, that's what it is.
I need evidence

There is something to be said about the process of using your hands to put something together, to handwrite a letter and drop the package in the mailbox. It takes a different level of thoughtfulness and deliberation than the immediacy of, say, the Internet.

Things I learned about through zines:

bell hooks

Obscure trivia about a slew of indie rock bands that released 7" records and then disappeared off the face of the earth

Comics

Emma Goldman

The useless beauty of a sheet of vellum

Gentrification

Herbal abortion

Nikki Giovanni

The ingenious efficiency of a long-armed stapler

Linoleum block printing

Pabst Blue Ribbon

How to maximize a single sheet of paper to make odd-sized zines

Brooklyn

The Magnetic Fields

How to sheath your stamps in a layer of glue so that the recipient can wipe off the postage ink and reuse them

The subtle but fundamental difference between a real typewriter and a computerized typewriter font

Sleater-Kinney

Making the most out of a Greyhound trip

Pen pal etiquette

The word "outro"

How to make envelopes using pages torn from a magazine

Yes, the personal is political, and just as I had always hoped, there really was another world out there.

I figured out that there was no need to swallow up my words when there were people out there craving them, or something like them.

So, we should make things. You should. Make zines using scissors and paper and pens. Even if the zines eventually get thrown away or if they're a little embarrassing or if there's some bad spelling in there, it's okay. That part doesn't matter. What matters is the importance of having tangible evidence and amassing proof.

We should make things that we can keep around for later, even if just to burn them.

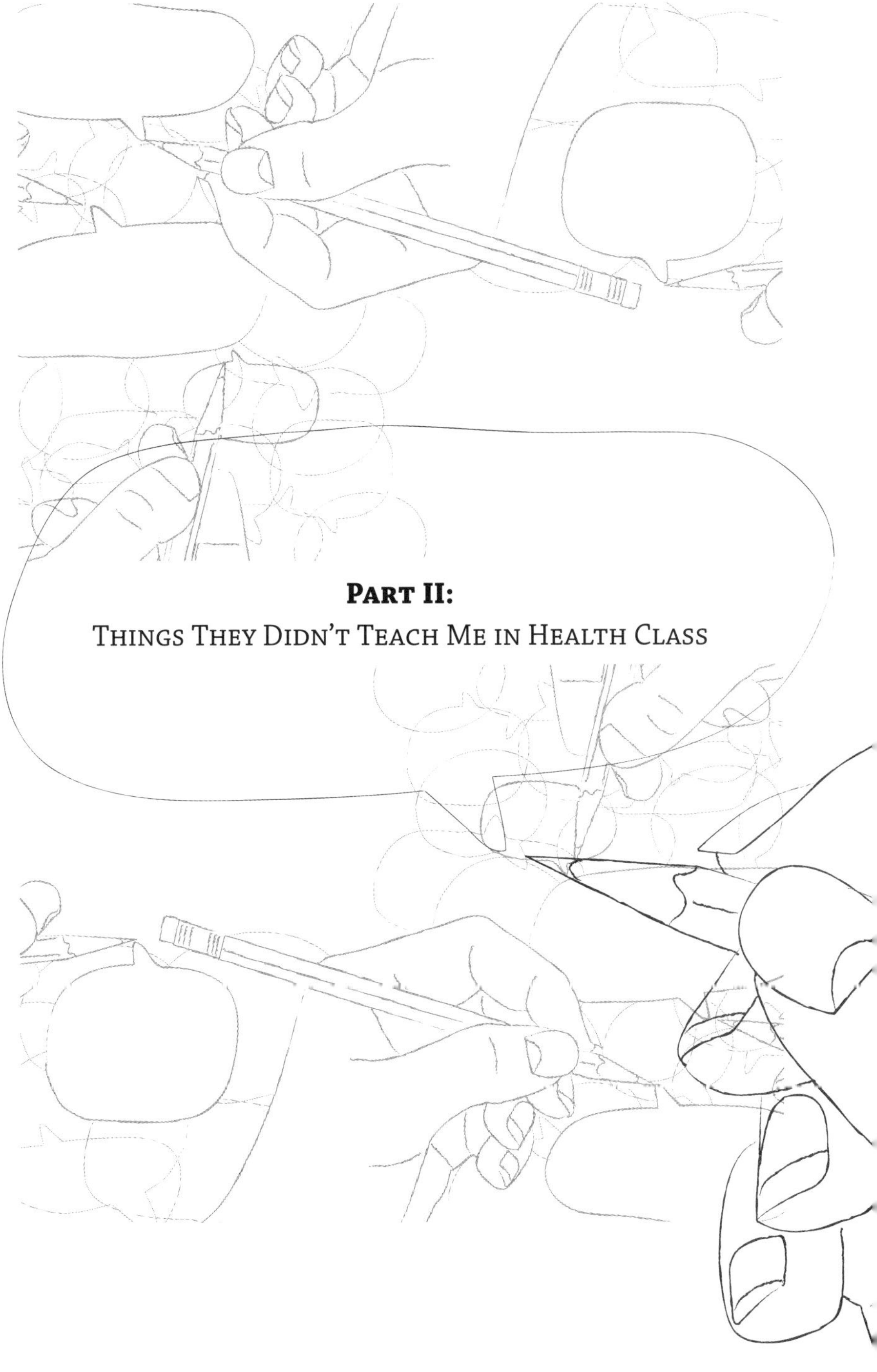

Part II:
Things They Didn't Teach Me in Health Class

Flat

Shannon Gerard

SHANNON GERARD

FLAT

it WAS HALF MAGIC
AND HALF DULL ACHING

i SPENT EACH OF MY HIGHSCHOOL SUMMERS WORKING AS A CAMP COUNSELLOR AND FOR TWO MONTHS EVERY YEAR, THE REGULAR EXPERIENCE OF MY LIFE FELT AMPLIFIED

WHAT I LOVED WAS HOW THE CLEANER AIR OF ONTARIO'S MUSKOKAS ALWAYS MADE ME FEEL HUNGRIER,
HOW THE PARTICULAR LENGTH OF SHADOWS AT 6PM IN AUGUST ALWAYS MADE ME WISH FOR HOME,
AND HOW I ALWAYS SLEPT BETTER UNDER THOSE DEEP, WIDE SKIES
FULL OF STARS.
THERE WAS ONLY ONE DENT IN AN OTHERWISE BLITHE EXPERIENCE....
BOOBS
OR, MORE PRECISELY, MY DRAMATIC LACK OF BOOBS.

COMPOUNDED BY RED HAIR AND WHITE SKIN (A COMPLEXION FOR WHICH MY MOTHER PACKED SUNSCREEN SO STRONG WE CALLED IT "LIQUID SHIRT"), MY FLAT CHEST MADE WEARING A BATHING SUIT AN UNCOMFORTABLE PROBLEM.

SMALL BOOBS WOULDN'T HAVE BEEN SO BAD IF IT WASN'T FOR MY OTHER ADOLESCENT TROUBLE — BOYS.

WHERE WERE THE GIRLS FROM "FACTS OF LIFE" WHOSE BREASTS I HAD SO EARNESTLY LOOKED UP TO AS A CHILD?

WHERE WERE JO, BLAIR, NATALIE AND LITTLE TOOTIE

NOW?

I COULDN'T ESCAPE THE SUSPICION THAT IF I HAD BOOBS, I'D SOMEHOW BE COOLER... THAT ALONG WITH CLEAVAGE, I'D BECOME POSSESSED OF THE SOCIAL EASE THAT HELPED OTHER GIRLS – GIRLS LIKE BLAIR – GET WHAT THEY WANTED.

BUT UNLIKE TV STEREOTYPES, IN WHICH THE BOOBLESS DUCKLING TURNS INTO A BEAUTIFUL SWAN AND THE FLOUNCY BLONDES END UP PREGNANT AT 20, I'VE SINCE WATCHED MOST OF MY OWN BLAIRS GROW UP INTO INTELLIGENT, SUCCESSFUL WOMEN.

THEY ARE HAPPY NOW AS THEY WERE THEN.

AM I?

A Little Lesson in Lust

K. Bannerman

"Look what I found!"

Her eyes sparkled as she reached into her backpack, pushing aside rumpled math homework and a couple of crumpled comics. I didn't know what to expect—an injured crow found in the ditch on the road to school? Her first training bra, bought by her mom? A tube of lipstick grabbed from the drug store bargain bin?

Out came a book: tattered, worn, with a cover the colour of nicotine-stained skin. She put it on my desk, and we huddled close, all four of us, a quartet of girls no older than twelve. The year was 1986, grade seven, and we found ourselves staring at the scantily clad silhouette of a voluptuous woman, a riding crop clenched in her hand. My best friend had rescued it from the trash bin behind the public library, where it had doubtlessly been chucked by a prudish librarian.

In oppressive black font, the title read, *Lady of Lust*, by Carlotta Baker.

In the mid-eighties, there was no Internet. My town was small. At the age of twelve, I didn't even know the word *pornography*. Still, studying the book in front of me, I knew this was not the sort of genre included in my high school's English curriculum.

The title character was the Sapphic manager of an office building, who hired buxom young girls for various forms of employment. Don't ask me what her business did because, frankly, I didn't notice. The author might not have even included it, obviously it wasn't important to the plot. The girls were hired as secretaries, but they did more than make coffee and take memos.

In the weeks that followed, my friends and I surreptitiously passed that book from one to the other, underlining phrases we didn't understand and words we couldn't find in the dictionary. *Lady of Lust* became our codex to all things adult and mature, the key to worlds beyond our imaginations, and it introduced us to a universe of delights that, to our adolescent minds, seemed brutal and puzzling. Why would people enjoy being spanked? Did all office managers have a selection of handcuffs and chains in their desks? And where were all the men? The world of sex and business seemed to be populated by crowds of women who liked wearing rubber panties under their tight skirts and whacking each other on the bottom with paddles and narrow belts. Truly, adulthood promised to be a daunting place, but it tantalized us, so full of exotic rites of passage that lay beyond rational comprehension.

Not only did we read *Lady of Lust*, but we strove to emulate its dime-store style, churning out our own erotic (but naive) tales. We would gather together after school and read our creations aloud, tittering over naughty phrases, parading our defiant use of nasty curse words with chins held high, and trying to disgust each other with the gooey biological intricacies of copulation. We talked dirty. We rebelled in the only way we knew how—by writing, and creating, and exploring with words a world that was not yet ours to traverse.

I was terrified that my mother would find my foolscap pages. After sharing each story with my three friends, I would take it, seal it in an envelope, and burn it in the rusted barrel at the back of our property. I'd watch the smoke curl around the words, the black soot creep across the white, and words disappear into ash.

Then I'd go back to my desk and write another, and another, and another. Erotica became a strange ritual, fraught with anxiety and cleansed with fire. When I needed inspiration, I would return to the finger-worn pages of *Lady of Lust*, the First Lady of literature, our leather-clad muse. She perplexed us, but she spurred a passion in our hearts (and maybe even spurred something else, a little farther down).

I don't remember any other book I read in grade seven. I'm certain there were others, but *Lady of Lust*, with its pages of soft-core lesbian erotica, swept all other novels aside. I ask you: faced with rubber panties and bullwhips, how could my stuffy high school English curriculum possibly compare?

Vaginal Discharge

Jessica McGann

In 1987, I was eleven years old going on thirty. One day I wanted nothing more than to hang out with my mom and watch Disney movies, and the next I was watching music videos and muttering swear words in fervent whispers, like the prayers of a crazy person. My focus shifted entirely from the fantasy world of my childish mind (populated with fairies and ponies and rainbows and candy) to the physical world of my childish body. My pituitary gland, powered by mystery time-release forces, woke up like a sleeping giant and began bathing my neurons in hormones. My vagina, formerly only vaguely associated with toilet activities, began rumbling to life, as if a little person had woken up in there and started moving about, turning on lights and pulling levers. The whole thing began to whir and hum, making me preoccupied with the changes that were occurring, or anticipated after eye-opening sex ed classes. Freud would probably tell you that I had reached that key stage of psychosexual development, *the genital stage*.

Whatever it was, I sensed, with the timeless wisdom of human evolutionary instinct, that my mojo was rising

Is there anything more endearing than the precocious self-possession of the pre-pubescent girl? God, what I wouldn't give to see myself now as I saw myself then: physically flawless, most assuredly a genius, and certainly the envy of all my peers. I remember looking in the mirror and being absolutely astounded by my own beauty. My eyes took in my body (my matching fleece sweatsuit, my enormous piano-key teeth, and my stringy unwashed hair), processed the image through some kind of magic Child's Perception Machine, and churned out Taylor Dayne. I was completely unable to envision a time when people would compliment me, and I would disagree with them by pointing out my flaws. No way. I was perfect. Totally stunning. Ten long red nails away from being an extra in a music video.

And as soon as boys started noticing this too, they would certainly clamour for my mature lady charms.

There was a boy in my grade six class that I'd had a crush on since grade four. Everybody knew it—including the lucky fellow, I'm sure—and the fact that he never addressed it, or me, was not in the least bit discouraging. I just assumed he didn't know I was interested. Besides, even if he loved me back with all the intensity of grown-up passion, what would we have done about it anyway? I knew about sex, and that boys should want to have it with me, but only in a theoretical way. Actualizing these concepts was beyond me; it didn't even compute.

Or rather, it didn't compute until 1987. With the onset of reproductive capacity, Mother Nature was beginning to put it all together for me. I woke up one morning with an unfamiliar nether-region dampness. "Something happened in my underpants," I announced matter-of-factly to my mother, pulling them down to have a look. It wasn't blood, and it wasn't pee, and my mother didn't seem too concerned, or eager to talk about it. "You're getting older," she said vaguely, "it's normal." I went to school pleased that something older and normal had happened, but with no idea what it was. Fortunately, it was sex ed day at school.

We sat in little groups in my class, four desks pushed together like we were little patrons at a busy restaurant. My crush and I sat side-by-side facing two girls: Debbie, who wore a bra, and Nancy, who was the most popular girl in our class. We had just started our sexual education, and a special teacher came in once a week for these titillating lessons. Because I had been taught all about the birds and the bees at the tender age of three by my vigilantly regretful single mother, I anticipated these classes with a particular enthusiasm. It was my time to shine. I knew what penises were for, and how babies developed, and I was keen to show off my knowledge whenever possible. I nodded knowingly and sagely during the teacher's explanations of the basics, watched the videos with the blasé mien of someone who's heard it all before, and raised an are-you-serious eyebrow when we were encouraged to ask questions.

But the fateful day of the damp underpants, I did have a question: *Why do my underpants sometimes get wet at night?* I wrote on a scrap of paper. I dropped it into the anonymous question box with pride. As far as my peers knew, it could be about anything. Maybe I was asking for tips.

"Vaginal discharge!" exclaimed the teacher, when it was time to read the questions from the box. She scrawled the words out on the chalkboard in her beautiful, loopy cursive. She explained that it was a perfectly normal, healthy, sexually mature thing to experience. Beaming, I copied the words down in my notebook, hoping my crush would notice my telltale interest. In her attempt at assuaging youthful fears and establishing sexual equanimity, our teacher made vaginal discharge sound like a veritable hallmark of healthy, nubile sensuality. Nature's bat mitzvah. And I, eager that my crush should know that I was as ripe as a peach just waiting to plucked off the branch, leaned towards him and said knowingly: *"That happened to me last night."*

You know how some moments carry so much impact in such brief spaces of time that they burn themselves onto your cerebral cortex the way a bright light burns itself onto your retina, leaving a shadow in your vision long after you've looked at it? That's what this moment is for me. When I think about it, every detail springs clearly and easily to mind, even after all these years: our little desks with the storage underneath, their surfaces broken by years of compass and pencil etchings; my crush's boyish, freckled face as I leaned in towards him; Debbie and Nancy in profile, facing the chalkboard; those big schoolhouse windows behind them, lofty and dusty, framing the grey autumn sky beyond. That's what the first part of that memory is, the quiet before the storm. I see myself opening my mouth—oh, the horror! If only I could stop it now!—and then I can feel the burning heat of shame that seared through me seconds after I'd spoken. It seemed such a delicious, sexy thing to say before I had actually said it. Even now, with perfect clarity, I recall Nancy and Debbie turning towards me in unison, their faces contorted with disbelief. I can picture, as though it were yesterday, my crush's freckles dissolving in the angry red blush that rose up from his collar, and how his eyes darted wildly like a horse that's caught the scent of death.

Nancy, our unspoken leader, uttered the fatal, one-word judgment:

"Ew."

All of vaginal discharge's womanly merit was instantly negated. One minute I had been a sensual, brazen Lolita, and the next I was the grubby kid who was always being told by her mother to "think before you speak." Anna Nicole Smith 1992 to Anna Nicole Smith 2002 in one heartbeat. I turned towards the chalkboard with a sudden, intense interest, nonchalantly flipping over the page of my notebook to conceal my enthusiastic writing: "vaginal discharge!" Nancy and Debbie continued to stare, too stunned to look away.

I stared hard at the chalkboard, running damage control scenarios through my mind with typical eleven-year-old logic. I made a quick mental list of local schools I could possibly transfer to. I brainstormed follow-up conversations with my crush: "I thought she said something else!" I thought of grown-up lady rock stars and wondered if they'd ever said anything stupid when they were kids. Did Taylor Dayne ever discuss the distasteful secretions of her private parts with the kids in her class? Did Madonna? Were their vaginas as dry as their blonde, over-processed hair? As pristine as Nancy's white polo top, or Debbie's brand new bra? Or did they, too, wake up from pleasant dreams and need to change their underpants?

How quickly we learn at that young age. No lengthy discourse could have taught me about the perceived inappropriateness of discussing my body's functions as succinctly as that two-letter word: *Ew*. Right up until I became sexually active, I worried about what was going on in there. Was it weird? Normal? In girl's underpants all around me—on the subway, on the street, in line at the theatre—were the same things going on? I didn't fully understand the workings of the vagina until I actually started putting my vagina to one of the primary uses for which it was intended—despite all I'd learned about it from my mother's early efforts and my public school education. Like most sophisticated machinery, it was impossible to appreciate the genius of it until I actually used it. That's the beauty of the human body. Nature, like mothers everywhere, knows things that we'd never figure out as children. Sadly, intelligent design was the farthest thing from my mind that grey autumn day. I prayed that a devastating school bus accident would kill Nancy and Debbie and permanently damage my crush's short-term memory. And all the while, inside, hormone production was chugging along right on schedule. My reproductive organs were preparing for adulthood; my vagina was going about its business with blithe indifference to the day's humiliation. Inside, a mutiny was brewing.

That was the day, I suppose, when I really began to understand that I was supposed to be ashamed of my body. There wasn't anything grown-up and amazing about my vagina, or anyone else's. *Vagina* was the grossest of all the anatomy words; even penis was less cringe-worthy. From grade school, we went on to junior high, where I learned that vaginas smelt bad. In high school, I learned that they looked nasty, like wounds. Periods and cramps could be talked about, but tampons and pads remained a mortifying purchase, and the sight of a single drop of leaked menstrual blood could make a girl untouchable for years to come.

Vaginas are the elephant in the room. We sexualize girls for their breasts and their bums as if that were the sum total of their physique, when the real, amazing part of a woman's sexuality is her vagina. Enlightening though my mother and the public school system were, it was *Cosmo* magazine that taught me that the vagina has muscles. This was news to me. I thought of it more as a thoroughfare: penises in, babies out. I had been using my vaginal muscles to hold things *in*, in a ridiculous effort to keep my panties dry, or maybe to just make my vagina disappear altogether, but I had never thought of it as a muscular exercise. I had never thought of my vagina as something that could be strong.

Now, as an adult, I talk about my vagina all the time. Maybe I'm sort of smitten with it, this amazing piece of biological machinery. Maybe it just gives me a delicious thrill, saying a quasi-dirty word. Everybody winces at the V-word, but there is also always this relieved laughter. Like they're glad somebody finally said it. Say it with me now, Nancy and Debbie: We have vaginas! Isn't that wonderful? Messy and compelling, sexy and bizarre, my vagina is the Taylor Dayne of my anatomical components. Producer of babies, pleasure, and that glorious herald of sexual maturity—discharge. It takes a lot more than two-letter words to keep me from telling boys about it now.

Oh, Go Eat A Hamburger

Shaunga Tagore

Just because my ass is bony doesn't mean I have an eating disorder.

Yeah sure, being this twig-thin has its drawbacks. My wrists are too flimsy to ever win a battle against a tight-lidded jar of strawberry jam. And I still cringe when I remember arm wrestling in elementary school gym class, everyone crowded around, betting how fast my opponent-of-the-moment could take me down.

But if you want to know what really turns my stomach, consider this conversation with Nellie, my middle school best friend. We were in the cafeteria at lunch, enjoying our mom-made sandwiches.

Nellie says to me: "You're anorexic."

"Whaaa?" I reply with my mouth full, lettuce caught between my teeth, bacon hanging out of the side of my mouth.

"You're anorexic."

I chew for a few moments, gulping down my sweet, juicy pig.

"No, I'm not," I say.

"Yeah you are. You're too skinny."

"Buuut . . . I like eating. I eat all the time."

"Doesn't matter."

"But I just said . . ."

"I don't care. You're sooo anorexic."

Really. How can you argue with that?

Of course, even if I'd had an eating disorder, this conversation still wouldn't have been a divine eye-opening experience. You know, like:

"You're anorexic. Eat a hamburger. Get over it."

Or not.

Every single TV show I watch, magazine I flip through, or music video I groove along to, tells me that in order to be truly attractive and desirable, I need to be part of the tall, thin, big-boobed, small-hipped, blonde-haired, and blue-eyed masses. But instead of passing judgment on others, I would prefer to spend my time enjoying fresh-from-the-oven nachos with green onions, tomatoes, and cheese!

You want to know something crazy? Last year when I visited my family in India for the first time, I realized something: I am actually AVERAGE HEIGHT AND SIZE. I didn't have to crane my neck to have a conversation with my uncle, and I could easily borrow my cousin's clothes. I strolled down the packed, cluttered streets of Kolkata, and suddenly realized that I was no longer the scrawny, malnourished, poor, starving brown girl in a white-dominated Canadian high school. I wasn't a freak or abnormal, I wasn't automatically the subject of anyone's pity. I was just *me* . . . and there was absolutely nothing wrong with looking like me.

I came home to Canada, beaming with newfound liberation. But soon enough, I had an unfortunate visit from a well-intentioned Avon lady.

"You could be really pretty you know, you just need to *eat* more. You should *love* yourself, you know? Get rid of that low self-esteem!"

Low self-esteem? Lady, I wouldn't trade in this brown skinny bod for some blonde Barbie-doll figure any day. When I'm fifty, I'll probably still be able to find clothes in the kid's section. My boobs will never be big enough to make it onto the cover of *Cosmo*—and I like it that way.

So, next time you tell me that I must be anorexic because I am simply too skinny for my own good, you better watch out. Because I'm going to *sit* on you. And with my incredibly bony ass—you bet it's gonna hurt.

SHE WILL ARRIVE

Karma Waltonen

She will be here in a few moments: the friend, but "not girlfriend" of my fourteen-year-old son.

This is horrifying.

"You were only a few years older when I knocked you up," e-mails his father to make me feel better.

It has the opposite effect.

When I was fourteen, I went over to a boy's house. We were in his mother's very formal dining room—trying to talk, which was harder in person than over the phone. I was wearing a dress my mother thought was appropriate for church and, at my grandmother's insistence, a hand-me-down slip. During one of the awkward pauses, the elastic of the ancient slip snapped. The faux silk half-slip slid down and caressed my ankles. Just as I was picking it up and balling it into my hand, the boy's mother came into the room.

"Is that your slip?"

"Yes," I said, the picture of nonchalance.

I was never invited over again.

I am mortified for this girl and what might befall her. Embarrassed completely for my son, before he knows how bad it can get.

One of my high school boyfriends shoplifted condoms because he was too ashamed to buy them—he worried that the store owner, a stranger, would call his parents. The one night we had sex, we had to three times. There were three condoms.

She will arrive and I will be reminded of how young I am, ever the imposter around other people's children. Other people who were independent when they decided to have children, rather than having independence and dependents thrust upon them.

She will arrive and I will be reminded of how old I am. She will giggle incessantly, and I will be sure I never did that. I will stop myself from cringing.

She will arrive and be much shorter than my son, who is already taller than I am.

She will arrive and be a picky eater, like my son. They will be polite, but not polite enough to eat whatever it is they object to, as is the custom of their generation. She will consume one and half pieces of ham for dinner. I will worry that her parents will be able to tell when they pick her up that she is malnourished and that it is my fault.

She will arrive and be more confident than I was at her age. She will not be shy—she will tease my son. When he teases back, she will say, "You're so sarcastic."

He will reply, "I learned it from her," and point to me.

I will smile and confirm this.

At some point, I will cuss in front of her. She will pretend she doesn't mind, but I won't be sure.

She and my son will constantly be touching each other. They will berate the other in a way that necessitates one hitting the other. They will wrestle. I remember this. This is their only way to touch—to pretend to constantly be fighting. They aren't sure how else to. They aren't sure why they want to.

After she leaves, she will call him two more times that night and he will scuttle off to his room to talk to her.

She will arrive soon. I am in the kitchen cooking dinner and pretending to be a grown-up. I am in jeans and a tank top. I have put on a bra just for her. My son comes up behind me. He grabs the bra strap that has fallen over my shoulder and jerks it back up. "Mom," he says, exasperated, "can't you be decent?"

It's still all about my underwear.

Part III

Getting Grounded: Run-ins with Authority

The Other Side

Denise Reich

It was better on the other side of the wall. That was the thought that drove me.

It was the winter of 1989, I was twelve years old, and I was halfway through my first year of junior high school. We couldn't go outside for physical education classes any longer because it was too cold, so we were banished to the confines of the gymnasium. An accordion screen divided the gym in two, and the students were segregated along with the space. On one side of the barrier, the boys played hockey. On the other, the girls square-danced.

Could we play hockey? The question was dismissed without a second thought: *Why would you want to play with the boys? They might bump into you! It's far better to dance!*

We glared at the gym teacher, Ms. E., with sour eyes as she brushed off our protests.

There was no attempt to teach us anything; we were simply herded into ornery groups of four and forced to do-si-do for a half hour. Ms. E. didn't even show us the dances; she just turned on a record, sat down on the sidelines, and immersed herself in her marking book. We were doing the seventh grade version of Simon Says.

Occasionally when someone slipped or turned the wrong way we giggled, but for the most part, our eyes stayed focused on the floor and our faces were frozen into grim frowns. We dreaded going to the gym every day. As we trudged around in staggered, unenthusiastic circles, we knew it was all a waste of time.

Every now and then, when the record ended and we were momentarily spared the sound of the screeching banjos, we heard the sounds from the other side of the gym. There were whistles, and shouts from the male gym teacher, and sneakers squeaking against the polished wooden floor. I could occasionally hear the hockey sticks clicking.

I was aware that on the other side of the screen, my male classmates were learning something exciting and interesting. I was aware that I was not. And then the record would start up again and I'd shuffle back into line.

My classmates let it go when we were out of our gym clothes and back in the hallways. I didn't want to. It simply wasn't fair. I wanted to learn to play hockey instead of walking in circles. I didn't want to be shut out of an activity because I was a girl, and I didn't want to forget about it.

My friend Nee wrote a column for the school newspaper. When we rode the city bus home together one afternoon, she proudly showed me the latest issue. It dawned on me that I didn't know how to protest, but I did know how to write.

I went home and dashed off a biting editorial that was one part frustration, one part anger, and one part sheer resentment and hurt that I'd had to spend a month and a half not playing hockey. I signed it with my initials and sent it to the editors by way of Nee.

I didn't hear about it again for a month. Had it been published? Had it been laughed at and tossed into the bin? The teachers received the new editions of the paper before we did, and it was Ms. E. herself who alerted me to my article's publication.

We were sitting in the auditorium, waiting for an assembly to begin, and with all the activity, I didn't see Ms. E. until she was standing right in front of me. She smiled, leaned down and pinched my cheek hard enough to hurt.

"Did you write that article in the *Pasteur Eyes*?" she said, low enough that only I could hear the words. I swallowed hard and said no, of course not. She knew I was lying, I knew I was lying, and I knew there was no way I was going to escape a conversation with her.

Of course, calling it a "conversation" is a bit of a stretch. It was a roast, and I was on the skewer. For the next several minutes I squirmed in my seat, and my sympathetic classmates did their best to appear completely oblivious, while Ms. E. offered her most candid comments on my article. The records weren't old, she told me. They were brand-new. Most of the girls didn't have a problem with square dancing. Why did I? I looked down at

Special Report-Unfairness in Gym

By D.R.

Denise Rieck

I think there is an injustice in the 7th grade gym class. While the girls play tennis, basketball, and square dancing, the boys play football, hockey, and basketball.

Why can't boys and girls play basketball together? And why must we square dance, when the boys have a chance to play hockey? I see no reason for this prejudice. If everyone learned basketball and hockey together, then there would be time for another sport. The same objective would be accomplished and the girls would not have to make fools of themselves square dancing.

Does the staff think we enjoy square dancing? First of all, it's not really useful, since nobody even square dances anymore. Does anybody square dance at the Pasteur dances? Secondly, almost all the girls, including myself and my entire gym class, despised doing the steps, making fools of ourselves, and listening to some old hillbilly guy on a 50-year old record. Hey, this isn't some little country town!! This is New York City!

Although for all the seventh graders this torture is over, I hope the school will consider making the gym program more egalitarian and fair for all future students.

the floor, willing myself to vanish. I couldn't respond. I'd already said all I needed to say.

Did it have an impact? Ms. E.'s reaction was volatile enough to lead me to believe that it did. I'll never know what transpired. What I do know is that after the scratchy records were put away, we were informed that we would be learning indoor hockey. We bounced around the gym, brandishing our sticks and chasing after the ball with far more zeal than we'd ever put into our do-si-dos. People were smiling. There was laughter. Ms. E. was grim as she saw our joyful and determined side, the one that revealed itself when presented with the challenge of an activity we truly wanted to learn.

Ms. E. didn't forget my editorial, of course. She carried the grudge into the next school year. In our annual physical fitness assessment, I placed well in the races and did more sit-ups than anyone else in my group, but somehow managed to avoid winning a single certificate. The year before, with far worse results, I'd received two.

It didn't matter. Ms. E. had not appreciated my commentary but the two teachers who advised the newspaper had, and they asked me if I'd like to write more articles.

In September, just as my time in the 50 metre dash was mysteriously misreported, I was named one of the editors of the newspaper. By January, members of the community school board were sending the principal complimentary letters about my work. Two years later I received my first byline in a mainstream adult publication.

The noise on the other side of the wall is still there, of course. These days it's louder, and ruder, and more critical, and I'm still writing about it.

Dear Monsieur Giroux

Dianah Smith

Dear Monsieur Giroux,
Remember me? I sat beside Claire Connell in your grade four French class at Queen Elizabeth Public School. I was also in your grade two and grade three French classes—after Madame Letourneau got married and left our school after grade one. I didn't like her anyway. She forced me to stand at the front of the class with gum on my nose just because I was chewing gum in class. She always picked favourites and was mean to the rest of us. On the last day of school, she showed us her wedding pictures. She was wearing a beautiful white dress, she had flowers in her hair—all the pictures were taken in a garden. She looked beautiful. I hardly recognized her. That was the only time she let us talk during French class. Otherwise it was *Silence!*

I liked when you came to our school. Because of you I was good in French again. I was good at conjugating verbs:

Je suis
Tu es
Il, Elle, On est
Nous sommes
Vous êtes
Ils/Elles sont

I loved all the words that were so boring in English but sounded funny in French. Words like *pamplemousse, parapluie, pomme de terre.* I was good at learning new words and I practised them as much as I could because I wanted to beat Maxine in our weekly vocabulary test. We had lots of fun making up stories in class and putting on skits. When you came back from March Break one year you looked like a lobster. At least that's what everyone else said, but I had never actually seen a live lobster before.

One afternoon, we were sitting on the carpet at the front of the room working on a group activity. I was wearing a yellow sweater with a loose neck that hung low. I had worn it many times before. You walked around to check on our group. As you stood above me you looked at me and then looked into my top and back in my eyes. Your expression was different, I didn't recognize you, and you smiled as if we had a secret. Your thick mustache twitched just a little, but most of the change was in your eyes.

I didn't like our secret. I felt different but not special. I didn't want to conjugate verbs or practise my vocabulary anymore. I didn't care if Maxine won the next vocabulary quiz.

That afternoon you changed from one of my favourite people to a stranger that I didn't recognize. You taught me the words for love, laughter, and friendship but I had not learned the words for betrayal or loss of innocence.

Red Bars

Catherine Graham

I was sitting in the backseat, fingering the silver seatbelt, half-listening to Mom and her friend Eleanor. We were taking the back route, the safe route, to the mall, instead of the highway, so Mom wouldn't make those sharp intakes of breath (no transport trucks to pass us). Still, she seemed high-strung, her mouth tight as she nodded in response to Eleanor's yammering.

Start of another season of swim classes. I was trying for my Bronze Medallion this time round and my green Speedo left indents on my shoulders. Red bars.

With both hands on the wheel, Mom was oblivious to me watching her. I stared at the squiggles congregating on her nose, red like her hair.

Her hair had grown back soft and thin, in opposition to Eleanor's coarse, black spikes.

At Sears we managed to avoid the spray-attacks of the perfume ladies, and we were standing in the bathing suit section, when Mom veered us away. I hid the glossy black one that I wanted on a shelf and wedged myself through the clack of racks.

"What do you think?" Mom smiled as she held up a fancy nightgown. The neckline was bordered with baby blue cross-stitching, a simple yet intricate pattern. It made me think of ants, their bodies snipped and glued into complex shapes.

"Here. This goes with it," Eleanor said, holding its match. She pressed a long sleeve into my hand. The fabric was so bright I thought the bathing suit, the last thing I had touched, would leave a black mark.

"But will it be warm enough?" I said, touching it. "You get cold at night,

Mom." Even post-treatment, Mom still got the chills.

"Not for Rusty," Eleanor said, "for you."

Mom passed Eleanor the fancy nightgown and Eleanor held it up to my chest for Mom to see. After they nodded, I was told to look in the mirror.

The straps were the width of bathing-suit straps and the bodice was lined with piping a shade lighter than the blue of the intricate pattern. I couldn't help but think, *isn't this what women wear on their wedding night? Women with breasts?*

"I don't get it," I said and looked at Mom in the oval mirror. She was looking at my chest, her eyes wide and watery, as if filling in the gaps.

I went home that day with an expensive nightgown set, not the black Speedo bathing suit I wanted. So I crossed my arms as Mom drove us home. I put my head down and sulked.

The day of my Bronze Medallion exam I barely fit into my old Speedo. Elastic cut into all parts it touched.

I pushed the red out of my mind and I did what the examiner told me to do: I swam the full length of the Centennial Pool underwater. I breathed my Tic-Tac breath into the sour-smelling mouth of a bony boy. I saved two pseudo-drowners. All the while Mom, like the other moms, watched through the glass.

After the last rescue, the examiner huddled us into a corner. One by one, she called out the names of the students who passed. When she finished, we all stood up. We had to walk by the glass to get back to the change room, and because I was last in the line of six, I witnessed the high-fives and hand waves. The responses of the mothers were all the more manic. When I saw red, I knew Mom was watching me.

So?

I looked the other way.

Two weeks later, when the badge arrived in the mail, Mom congratulated me. By then she knew I'd passed, but I didn't tell her when she needed me to, standing there with the healthy mothers, waiting.

"Why didn't you tell me? Why?" She said this to me in the car at least three times; her voice had no anger in it. Again I fingered the buckle that strapped me in and watched my middle finger turn red.

"Look!" I said and pulled down the neck of my sweater. I touched the red bar on my shoulder only to find the red bar wasn't there.

Perhaps that's why, when she handed me the badge, I went straight to my room and threw it in the closet. Why I lay on my bed and turned on the clock radio. It muffled my outburst of tears.

Split

Pam Park Jost

I was adopted when I was six months old from Seoul, South Korea. Later, I was told that I cried during the entire flight from Seoul to North America, and all the way to my new house. I think even as an infant, I knew that something was askew, that my family was different from me. I knew that I didn't belong.

I grew up in a seashore suburban town, known for its horse farms and hicks: in other words, white suburban hell. Growing up, white people freaked me out, but later, I realized that other Asians did too.

I had three sisters and five brothers (including two other Korean adoptees, inspired by my dad's experience in the Korean War). I was the troubled child, the one with the attitude problem. My parents called me "spoiled," but I only dreamed about the one thing I couldn't have: my birth parents. My closest confidante was my sister—the other black sheep. Our parents called her a "druggie" and kicked her out of the house when she got pregnant. They told me she didn't love us and ran away.

I was barely a teenager when my oldest brother started commenting about my body. It was a constant barrage: he said I had a fat ass, "nigger lips," and a flat face. I didn't realize that he wanted to touch my ass, kiss those lips, and caress my face. I self-consciously tugged on my nose hoping it would grow, and held my mouth tight in the mirror so my lips didn't appear as large. A few years later, he got himself his own Asian girlfriend and left me alone.

I felt white. My friends were white. I liked what they liked and did what they did. We imagined that we were white rock stars: I was Chrissie Hynde, Beth was Stevie Nicks, Kim was Steve Perry, and Lisa was Geddy

Lee. Someone else was Joan Jett. I rarely saw other Asians, and when I did, I felt uncomfortable, freaked out, confused.

School was miserable. Other kids said, "Hey, look at the Chinese kid!" (but I'm not Chinese, I'm Korean). I wore hand-me-downs from my sisters that seemed like they were from an entirely different decade. I slunk along the hallway walls and hoped I was invisible. I pushed away any desire to understand my culture, my adoption, my internalized racism, and my difficult relationships with people. And to make things more complicated, I realized I was queer at the same time.

By the time I hit grade eight, I was severely depressed (prompting my Dad to give me the book, *How To Win Friends and Influence People*, which was useless). I was petrified of the racism that was part of everyday life at my public school, so my parents sent me to a private school where the class size was six. We were all rejects and outcasts. Richard was hyperactive and had issues with sexual boundaries. Billy was also adopted, and was tormented at his old school because his twin brother was mentally disabled. Jim had to leave public school because people beat him up and said he was gay. Grethel and Trina lived forty minutes away, in another scary white suburban town, where they were picked on because they were black. We bonded in our isolation, although there was something lonely about being segregated from the "normal" kids. I ended up hiding away, and it took a long time to return.

Some people have told me I am privileged to be adopted—adopted to North America and to speak English as my first language. I don't know what it is like to immigrate to another country, having to learn the language, be discriminated against because of an accent. I don't have the memory of a homeland and family members separated by politics and circumstance. Instead, I was torn from my country, history, and culture before I was old enough to choose. I've felt divided—neither genuinely Korean nor North American, separate, longing to return to the country where I was born, desperate in the desire to learn about the culture, language, and family that I've missed.

The last "family" dinner I went to was in August 2003, during my first visit to my hometown in two years or so. My oldest brother told jokes about "ragheads" and "little Mexicans," crouched down low so I couldn't hear. At the end, everyone laughed. I realized that I don't need to tolerate this any longer. I can adopt my own family.

Like many other adoptees, I returned to Korea as an adult. I wanted to recover a tiny fraction of the loss I'd always felt. Loss in different directions: trying to lose the loneliness I grew up with and trying to heal the loss of culture, language, family (what does that even mean?). In the process, there was so much to learn and unlearn and, for the first time, I gained a sense of my own existence. A strange sense of belonging.

Get Well Soon

Maggie Dort

My family doctor sent me to my first therapist because he thought I needed someone to talk to. Doctors don't have time to talk, so they fill out a form and send you to someone else. That's how it works. The therapist turned out to be a social worker whose office was in a strip mall, next to the laundromat. "Your doctor's really worried about you," she said. She spoke quietly like she was afraid she'd spook me. She let me pick my own chair and everything. I nodded. Yes, my doctor was very worried about me. I was fifteen and sullen. "Tell me about your family," she said. She had me draw a family tree. That's how she found out my mom was dead.

"Well that must have been hard on you, to lose your mother at such a young age," she said, but I don't remember it being that hard.

I remember my mother driving from Truro to Halifax for chemo every week, taking me with her to keep her awake. Our car was named Rust Bucket. When it rained it was my job to push the windshield wiper button. It didn't have any kind of low setting, just either on or off. I had to turn it on, and then off, and then on again. I remember thinking I was helping her drive.

To keep my mom entertained, I would have a singing contest with the radio. The radio would sing one song and I would sing a different song, which is harder than you think. I always sang Bob Marley and the radio always won. One night the muffler fell off and we drove home with our heads out the window. We managed.

When my mother was admitted to the hospital, I stayed with my best friend Kariann for three weeks. It was like a sleepover the whole time. We pretended we were sisters. We walked to school together and did our homework together and ate Kraft Dinner with wieners. Her parents took me to the hospital to visit my mother, and I watched *Full House* in the TV lounge. I made her a card that said GET WELL SOON in bubble letters. I drew a picture of her with a green face, sitting in a hospital bed.

One night, Kariann's father woke me up to tell me that my mother had died. I remember that I didn't go to school that day, and that everyone in my class made me a card. I remember the taxi ride to the funeral, but not the funeral itself. I remember my dad and step-mom renting a truck to bring all my belongings to their house. On the way we stopped at A&W for hamburgers.

I have gone through an awful lot of therapists, and it's not even because I'm particularly crazy. Partly it's because I don't like being judged by people who think they're smarter than me, but mostly it's because I never tell them the truth.

I became obsessed with the idea that they diagnose your illness based only on what you tell them. There are no blood tests or X-rays. Just talking. At first it felt like a tremendous amount of pressure. Everything I said was analyzed and became evidence. I tried my hardest to make sure everything I said was true. If I was asked how I felt about something, my answer always ended with "I think." But I got to the point where I realized I would never be able to articulate exactly what I was thinking and feeling, so I gave up trying and told them just enough to get the prescriptions.

One therapist had me do an exercise in self-exploration, as she called it. You write your name down the side of the page and think up a word that describes you for each letter.

I had done a similar thing in grade four for Father's Day. We wrote FATHER down the side of the page and framed the whole thing in Popsicle sticks. For R I put "radical." I didn't know what it meant, I just knew the Ninja Turtles said it when they talked about pizza.

For the therapist, I wrote:

M
A
R
G
A
R
E
Tired

I was just being a jerk, but she thought that I was genuinely having difficulty reviewing my inner self. She was very understanding. She said I could take it home with me and work on it some more.

I didn't go back to therapy until I was eighteen.

The first girl I ever kissed ran her hands over the scars on my arms and said, "Did your boyfriend do this to you?" We were in the hot pink bathroom of NRG, the first gay bar I'd ever been in. I went with friends, for the karaoke we said, and because they never ID. And this woman, drunk and probably, like, thirty-five, walked over to our table and told me that I was going to the bathroom with her. I followed her. When she kissed me, I didn't push her away.

"I would never do anything like that to you, baby," she said, leaning against the door of the stall. I didn't say anything. After years of making up lame excuses like cat scratches and cooking accidents, I'd started just not answering.

In my top drawer I kept a dull Swiss Army knife, a plain white lighter, and a little travel First Aid kit. The First Aid kit was my favourite. I liked the little cotton swabs with alcohol, and the clean white bandages. I would lay everything out and it was all so small and single-use and perfect.

For a few minutes, I would be totally concerned with this small act of taking care of myself. Nice square pieces of gauze, hypoallergenic tape, perfect concentration. Blood cleaned off the knife blade. Everything all fixed up nicely. But I didn't feel like trying to explain the complex reasoning behind it all to a drunk stranger.

I pushed her against the wall and kissed her. Hard. Her lipstick tasted like Halloween. I shoved my hips against her and kept my hands on her shoulders. She laughed.

Walking back to my table, I felt like everyone in the bar was looking at me. She followed me and sat with us. I noticed she was wearing a class ring and she told me it was from law school. She'd graduated the same year I'd entered grade three. She called me "baby" and kept touching me, asking me if I was sure my boyfriend wouldn't mind, trying to find out if I had one. I pretended not to hear her. I was terrified of her.

My therapist at the time told me that I don't really like girls. He told me I was confused. He asked me if I'd ever been sexually assaulted. He said I was disconnected from my environment and didn't know how to make friends. It made me want to shave my head and tattoo DYKE across my chest. It made me want to fuck his daughter.

I was back in therapy. Doctors always promised it would be helpful, they always told me the therapist or psychiatrist or whoever was very good. "He's very good," they would say as they searched through papers for a referral form. And I would say, "okay."

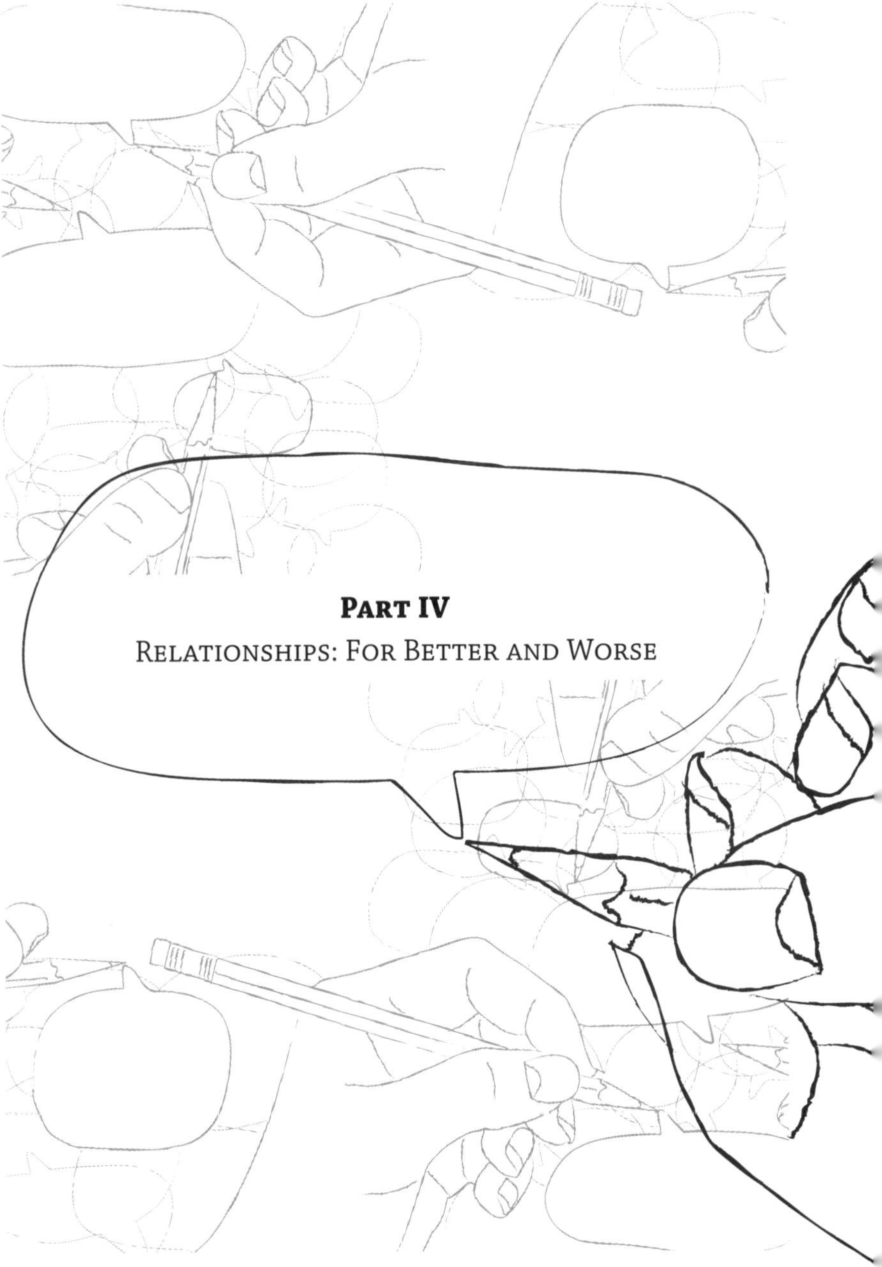

Part IV

Relationships: For Better and Worse

Ophelia Revisited

Julia Serano

We were more than just neighbours; we were practically best friends. And we would spend endless summer days together exploring the nearby woods, finding secret paths that led to landmarks only we knew about. And in the late afternoons we would hijack the playground two blocks away and turn seesaws into pirate planks, swings into trapezes, and monkey bars into towering infernos.

And some days we would both be wearing baseball caps and adults would joke that you couldn't tell us apart except for your ponytail. That was the only way to tell that I was the boy and you the girl. That was when we were ten.

Three years later, we were avoiding one another in junior high school hallways, our friendship shut off like a faucet as we sought the approval different cliques. And I saw you kiss your boyfriend hello at his locker each morning. No longer sporting baseball caps, you wore capri pants and spaghetti strap tops, and I watched you speak "I love you" to him in secret codes made up of hair twirls and perfectly timed eye blinks.

I got the distinct impression that he didn't speak your language.

But I did. I knew too much for my own good. I never told anyone this then, but I spent many sleepless nights wishing I were you. But junior high was no place for this transgendered tomboy to try to find herself, what with everyone acting out scenes from *Lord of the Flies* and unwritten rules like boys hold their notebooks at their side while girls cradle theirs against their chests. So I learned to settle for something less, like simply making it through the day without having anyone figure me out.

So I wore oversized flannel shirts to distort my slender body. Practised making stone-cold don't-fuck-with-me faces that convinced even the biggest pricks to leave the small kid alone. And in school, I excelled at science and math, because I knew that numbers and facts could never betray me the way my emotions could. I used logic as a shield, wielding my opinions like battle-axes at anyone who dared to get close to me. In other words, I turned into the cocky teenage boy that I was expected to be. But I would have traded it all to spend one day in your shoes.

And now, years later, I wonder if you felt the same way about me back then. Not that you wished you were a boy per se, but did you miss the part of yourself that would have liked to play stick ball, or take your rage out on my drum kit?

And I'm starting to think that the same thing happened to both of us. At the age of twelve we split ourselves down the middle, allowed to take only half into adolescence. You took the feminine, I the masculine, but we both sacrificed half a human being to the gods of fitting in. We both learned to say all the right things while biting our tongues, swallowing our pride, trying not to vomit up disgust. And we both hated our bodies for choosing our fates for us.

It took me twenty years to put the pieces of myself back together. And I'm still learning how to be both the giggling girl and the scientist. And I'm not sure what happened to you, but I like to imagine that you've managed to put yourself back together too.

I'm Still Here

E.J. MacBain

1982: Roller skates with rainbow knee-highs, braided friendship bracelets wet to the skin, blueberry Slurpees all summer from 7-Eleven, John Cougar cassette tapes of "Jack and Diane," the secret purple-clad, girls-only club, and threats from the older junior high school girls in the public library, who pretend that Crayola markers are boys' mini-dicks and suck them to show us: *This is what you have to do when you get to seventh grade.*

My parents' divorce, my mother's suddenly-single freak-out, the parties with her divorcée jet set, and her new *boyfriends, boyfriends, boyfriends,* while I sat with my friends and wondered about the state of their parents' love (and sex) lives and why the Girl Scout badges never fit, why I never graduated even from Brownies, and why all the boys loved all the girls who didn't look a thing like me, Kate, Heather, or Eve with her wicked thoughts and her slumber parties that turned to late-night viewings of the porn channel's *Midnight Blue.* What would Prince do? Who *was* Sheila E., and how could she be so sexy *and* play the drums? Why was the *Sports Illustrated* swimsuit issue so titillating, and why did my dad hide it? Were we the only ones who had to hunt so hard for soft-core porn?

Befriend Patty with her red polka-dotted headband and her pink-lined gym shorts with white cotton briefs. Spend every day from fourth grade on with her for two years. Visit her Army-barrack house and her Army friends, with all their toys littering the lawn and her long-haired mother in the dim kitchen with a bowl of brownie mix we dipped our fingers into.

Crave afternoons laying in her bed and the way the sun always stayed extra long on our skinny legs with their blossoming thighs. Count the tiny, tiny freckles from her ankle to the crease of her upper thigh—and my, oh my, how we promised to write each other forever when she had to move in sixth grade and then hugged so tight during our last goodbye before the bent-metal front door. We kissed a fraction of a second too long. I touched her hair like it was the silkiest ribbon from a stitched-up Strawberry Shortcake doll.

I love you, I said. *I love you, Patty—*

I love you, too.

The back of the classroom, where I camped out after the divorce. How come I hid out there? Why did I act that way? Blank stares from the teachers who don't understand why I don't understand and don't know why I didn't read the section, or can't understand why I just sit and write, but don't write anything about this assignment—just letters to Patty Strawberry-Shine Hair, Patty Finger in the Batter, and Patty Kiss at the Front Door.

Receive no letter from Patty five months later, but, still, write her every single day. Write all about the way the road just ends at the shore, and how you can't even imagine getting through a day here. What will happen now that Washington Junior High School is next, and what about the white cotton underwear? Are girls supposed to wear something else now; what is it about the swimsuit issue? Do you remember when we said goodbye?

Go back to the long hazy days. Find out that three girls have given blow jobs already. Say that the purple-clad, girls-only club should only allow in girls that don't wear tight designer jeans. *I mean, really, why do they do that?*

Remember the scene with Stacy when we played doctor and I made her look at me. No, *really* look. I asked her to use her stethoscope. And we did that—played—told each other that our butts were sick. *Yes, it's sick; you have to make it better.* Touch and kiss. See out the window the cars going by and then remember, it's now fifteen days to junior high. What will we do?

Remember that Patty still hasn't written, but that's all good. I can play doctor here with other girls. See her now on some other horizon—are her friends all tall like me? And do they wear their hair back like I do, in two tight barrettes? She's having fun with the Hula Hoop and jump rope, and she doesn't need to think about any of these things, like I do, here in the Northeast. I mean, she's in West Virginia now. They all picnic and sing gospel or something. None of them play Ms. Pac-Man. Or something. They all know that girls like Patty and girls like me can only play together without anyone noticing for so long, and then, you know, you have to say something to others about it, or, worse, you'll be taunted for what you do. You want to tell someone, like your mother. But see, your mother's in the bedroom now, wearing that slip as thin as a fly's wing, as slippery as sun-melted butter, and I can tell you, boyfriend number five is like boyfriend number three, except sometimes, somewhere, she comes out and sits with me, and tells me to prepare myself . . . *for everything.*

Cry all afternoon in the second-floor bedroom after realizing that Patty will never write back. Hurl old stuffed Curious George across the room and against the wall. Take the last remaining letter to Patty and tear it up for the trash can. Better yet, burn it in the toilet. You can't imagine what it might mean to look this close at a longing this shameful. Tell myself: *don't look too much, don't look too close.* Remember, it's not about the girls anymore even; it's about what you have to offer the boys.

Spend junior high school hiding in the girls' bathroom during all breaks.

Go to high school, but do it with barely a sound. Call for the boys, but barely make a noise. I said, *Hi.* I said, *Yes, I'm here.* I said, *No, I'm a friend of Claudia's. I belong here, really, can't you see?* She's the sexiest and prettiest girl at this basement-apartment-Jack-Daniels-post-hippie-band affair. Call me whatever you want to—pothead, silent girl, too-tall friend, the one looking too far back to the nineteen-sixties.

Go together everywhere. The three of us: Claudia, me, and Tori. Sexy, Silent, and Athletic. Broken, Broken, and Broken. Realize I can smoke it all till it makes us so silly, can't even imagine how we'll drive. Realize, though, that actually a guy sees me, and he plays the drums, too. Can't you hear this band playing "Dear Mr. Fantasy?" They practise over and over again then pray to the throne of Eric Clapton or Jimi Hendrix. They call this beat-up, Route-8 place the "Red House" and decorate the Christmas tree with empty whiskey bottles, then huddle in the back room for baked-up coke off cookie sheets. *Do I look OK?* I can't see so clearly in that bathroom mirror, and the line is so long while that boy cuts and snorts alone. *I look OK.* Timmy, the drummer, is here now. Wants to show me how he fixed up this old car. *Ride with me?* He asks. We go aimlessly. All the way to the beach. Slide down in the front seat so he can touch every part of me, and don't ask about the girlfriend at the University of Maryland or the other one crying upstairs somewhere in the Red House—see how quickly his fingers slide in, but don't part me all the way. Say, *I want to wait,* and then wait, every other day, a few more bases, till I can finally—*dear, Jesus*—let it all go. Why can't I just let it all go?

Cry for weeks too long after he finally leaves me, then weeks later have to write him that stupid letter: *I have chlamydia. Go to the doctor yourself, and tell those other girls.*

Try again with the too-skinny, too-scattered Justin, who always seems to have three, four, or five girls handy but is, thankfully, at another high school. We do it again and again, quickly, in his basement room, before he finds another stupid way to insult me. After sex, in the fluorescent-lit bathroom, he laughs at the stray dark hairs sprouting on my chest, and I vow to never open myself up that way with a stupid guy again. Don't ask them to look at your flaws. Remember, you only look that closely when you're alone. Remember how, somewhere, Patty is probably taller; remember to think more about the girls.

Stay with Claudia and Tori till we can talk all night, high, about sex. Remember to tell Tori to report our art teacher, Mr. Mitchell, who keeps leaving messages after school hours and telling her to come and meet him in that lot by Saugatuck Road, *just to talk.* Feel how nice it is to say: *I'm not a virgin.* Because really, this is what it was all about for so long. Those girls with their Crayola markers in the library just didn't know how easy it is to blow a guy.

Meet Thea at my after-school job. Find Ben, who lives in an apartment with Thea and Mike. They are all four years older than I am. Mike knows how to vandalize, and Thea understands me, because she left her own mother a long time ago. The four of us huddle and sigh. Ben is as silent as I am. But somehow, with them, we talk louder. Drink beer and sit cross-legged on the floor watching the sunset mark the window with its well-oiled brush. Realize that smart guys can actually be sexy, and notice how long I can actually keep the light on, and how much I can really say if I don't have to wonder if we are here just to fool around. I mean, I can do that, right? But then I can have deep sex and love, remember to think about not having one another for-*ever,* and then get scared—hard scared.

Have sex all the time and let him paint my portrait eighteen times over with two kittens running beneath our feet. Decide that, even though I'm failing, I don't want to be stuck in high school forever—I don't want to drop out and get high all the time, and give it all up just like that. Decide to be smart again, like Thea, and roll my own cigarettes and make my own jewelry and spend all fucking afternoon in the bookstore if I want and write letters to anyone who really pisses me off—and tell the men to stop staring and call the school to report Mr. Mitchell. But somehow, despite that, don't talk to my mother or to Ben about birth control, or say much about the first sexually transmitted disease. Don't think too far ahead. Remember to not look too close.

Go to the local bar and put money in the jukebox till the whole crowd knows how to overplay "Tupelo Honey." Don't think about the girls. Don't remember Patty. Remember my connection to Thea. Remember how she tells me how lovely I am—*so lovely*—all the time. *Let me hug you.* She loved all her girlfriends. They travelled and slept in patchwork quilts; they followed the Pixies even. They were crazy eighties girls. They talked all about their unplanned pregnancies and had abortions without apology. All their mothers were feminists. Just like Thea's. Just like mine. Remember to pull out the old *Ms.* book, *The Decade of Women,* when I get home, and trace my finger across those women again—those activists, those marchers, those fed-up suburban housewives, city workers, and students who said *fuck off* with just a T-shirt. They wanted equal rights *now.* Isn't that what made them all finally walk?

And here I am now, walking too—but still, tied to a guy. Here he is, too, worried about coming too fast, but not talking about it, or talking anymore about condoms or the Pill, and look at me, not talking about these things either. You wonder why it took a year to get pregnant.

Thea says, *I will help you.*

Ben cowers till he can't stop cowering. He tells me that he doesn't want me to keep it. He tells me that he does. He tells me things all the time when he's not reading *Howl* or drinking too much wine or threatening to go back to his college across the country now, for good, even though I've only just barely graduated high school and started college. He wants me to drop out, then, and move to Seattle. If I love him, then I will love him there. And if I don't, then I am "chicken." I convince myself that it's the "writer's life:" a crazy messed-up path—or, it's romance: I can walk blonde dogs and be blonde with a tiny blonde child, too. I can forget the fights and forget the loneliness and forget the books and forget the words—forget Thea, forget ever learning to agitate the world.

I call the clinic like I am joining some inevitable girls-only club. I call also to save my life. Really, I was weaned on choice. This is water to me; it's part of my birthright. That's why the women walked, and why I am here, why I fucked up. I had the right to fuck up. I didn't fuck up that bad; I fucked up bad.

At that first appointment, the doctor comes in to check me. She pushes down on my abdomen with one hand, and puts her fingers inside me with the other. She says, *Yes, you are pregnant.* She says to make the next appointment as soon as I can.

They counsel me before the procedure. Two women in the room. We sit around an oval wooden table. I am just nineteen, a long time from 1982. Patty is far from West Virginia. The chocolate batter is all dried up. The boys have gone home again; there are just women now. They look at me, but say few words. Ben is there, but he's not there.

He's not here, is he? They ask.

No. I am.

They tell me it's my choice, and one that only I can make. They tell me it's my choice, but it is one I will never forget—and I am here to tell you, that is the truth. The counsellors ask again, *Is this what you want to do?* I remember to tell them: *Yes, this is what I want to do.* This is it now; what do you think? I am nineteen years old, I am nineteen years old. I am not going to stay with him. I am not going to drop out of college. I am not going to *not* get my degree. Do I need to tell you how I just barely made it out of high school?

Ben drives the car the day of the abortion and cries again. He tells me to put his watch on and never take it off. Later, he says that the door that closed behind me was like the spinning-to-lock door of a submarine. He goes down with it. I stay numb.

The doctor's heels click on the linoleum floor. She says nothing to me. She aborts it quickly. It goes into that glass jar. Thea tells me later that the same thought I had had occurred to her—*it is done and it cannot be undone.* That is the choice, in black and white. That is the choice I made. That is the choice she made. The girlfriends know how to tell one another the stories—

and I walk back home to her, so she can tell me everything.

We sit and talk in her bed till the sun pushes another October day into sunrise, and she works her fingers over two thin needles with indigo wool. I go back to college and forget about Ben in stages. He kicks a hole in his painting of me with a pregnant belly and dumps our sand-sculpture-in-a-bottle all over the floor. I start a women's group and manage a campus magazine with story after story of feminist pride. I promise myself many things, but she was right: *I did not ever forget.*

Sometimes I still think of Patty and the freckles all up and down her legs. How many times did we lie there all quiet? Not a peep anywhere, from anyone. No one's hands on us, nobody's tongue—nothing to think about, really, except ourselves. That's how I always remember it. I don't even know now where she is—but I tell you, I know that I'm still here.

Looking for Normal

Jessica Lockhart

I found him in front of the pool hall, sitting with one of his buddies. *That asshole.* We were supposed to have plans. Slowing down in my dad's half-ton truck, I rolled down the window to give him the finger. No need to talk this out; gestures would have to say it all. But the hand motion was so foreign to me that my fingers formed the piece sign instead. *Dammit. Why can't I even be angry in a cool kind of way?*

For something with such innocent beginnings, I never thought it would turn out like this.

Okay, maybe not so innocent. We had only been dating for three days when he came home with me after the Valentine's-themed school dance. My parents were out of town for the week. I put on a turtleneck to keep warm, which he promptly took off. And then, ten minutes later, I was in my twin bed, staring at the ceiling. *How did I get here*? All I could feel was his left hip bone, digging into my flesh.

The first time he asked me out was in grade ten, right before spring break. "Do you know who Jason is?" my friend Michelle asked me. "He saw you during the pep rally and thinks you're really cute. I gave him your phone number. You're so lucky." When he called to ask me out, I said no. I wasn't into dating guys who I didn't know.

I forgot about the incident entirely until grade twelve. I had just broken up with my boyfriend of a year, Kenny, and the news was circulating. Jason's friends started hanging out at my locker and talking about him loudly. His female friends would come up and tell me, "He likes you, you know?" And every day when I pulled out of the school parking lot, I could see him smoking at the edge of the school grounds, staring at me. I was drawn to him. He was popular. He fit in. He was everything that I was not.

School was never easy for me. In a sea of Gap girls, my interest in politics and my fondness for black eyeliner, wigs, pink hair dye, and fishnets earned me the endearing nicknames "Satan" and "Psycho." Girls yelled: "Snap psycho! Snap! You know you want to!" and pushed me against lockers. They tripped me as I ran laps around the gym, making me fly into the wall; threatened to beat me up if I didn't transfer schools; spat at me whenever I walked across the school parking lot. Dealing with the administration was no easier—the principal admonished me for writing "anti-American" editorials in the school newspaper; the school counsellor told another student that I was a lesbian.

My town was far enough north that there was no escape. There was no hidden group of cool outsiders to intervene in the plot and save me; there were no secretly nerdy popular girls who wanted to give me a makeover and discuss books; there was nothing but 300 kilometers of barren, snowy fields in all directions. (My hometown didn't even get FM radio until 2005.)

The friends that I did have were fun and loyal: straight-edge kids who liked books better than beer. We drove around all night on empty highways and rented every musical at the video store. But I never quite found my place. *If you're strong enough to survive high school, you get into university.* At least that's the way I looked at it.

My friends regularly came to school with their wrists wrapped in scarves to cover the cut marks. Our after-school activities included making fun of the popular kids and me playing counsellor as they talked about their depression. But when I broke up with Kenny, they didn't bother to ask how I was feeling. I didn't complain because my problems seemed minor in comparison to theirs. And when he downed a bottle of Tylenol 3s, some of my friends blamed me. I felt like this heartless survivor who was being held solely accountable for the mental health of my friends and ex-boyfriend.

Jason seemed like a perfect alternative. He hung out with the popular kids, smoking at breaks and skipping classes. He played hockey and made out under the stairs. I pictured him buying me flowers and taking me to dances and never, ever discussing existential theories. And he was hot, hot enough that I couldn't believe he was interested in me. He would be the key to a completely normal high school experience.

So I said yes. And I—the token school freak, with good grades and perfect attendance—started dating the hot, popular kid from the wrong side of the tracks. The clichés only further convinced me that this would give me the normality I craved.

My parents saw things differently. They were livid. They warned me (in true made-for-TV fashion) that Jason had been in court more than once, that the reserve was dangerous.

"You need to watch your back," my mom said. "Those girls have threatened to beat you up more than once." She said it was just a trick. (Who did she think I was? *Carrie*?)

They tried to stop me. I accused them of being racist, of being bigots. They said I wasn't allowed to drive the truck on the reserve until the muddy roads dried up in June. That just made me more defiant. Jason didn't have a licence, but we always found a way. I'd drive the truck to the edge of the reserve and take a taxi the rest of the way, or he'd send one of his friends to pick me up.

I was infatuated. I was falling headfirst into the comfort of late night phone conversations and hand holding, and the excitement of breaking curfew just to cuddle in bed. Jason was sweet, and he truly cared about me. I'd sit huddled in flannel around a bonfire with Jason and his friends, and when the joint came my way, he would stand up for me. "She doesn't do that kind of stuff," he would tell everyone proudly. Suddenly, girls who wouldn't give me the time of day before wanted to be my friend. (I took glee in denying them this pleasure.) And people who had picked on me in the past, started to apologize. I loved my newfound notoriety.

My friends were less impressed. A couple of weeks into the relationship, they confronted me. "If you don't break up with him, we don't know if we can be friends with you anymore," they told me. "We always saw you as the strong one. We never thought you'd be so weak."

And they were right—I was weak. All of the strength I had gained as the defiant rebel was slipping away. I mean, I knew he was cheating on me. "Am I not good enough?" I wondered. I wanted to be the sexy, smart girlfriend. I didn't want to lose out to the girls whose phone numbers I found in his wallet. I tried to justify it to my friends. "I just want to know how it feels to have a normal high school relationship."

He bought me a dozen white roses and told me it would never happen again. When it did, I pushed him down a flight of stairs. (Granted, the flight was only three steps.) Somehow, he didn't get the message. I'd wake up to see his dark silhouette in my window in the middle of the night. He'd be drunk or stoned, and "just want to talk." One night, we got into a yelling match on the driveway, and my mom woke up. And that's how I found myself, at the age of eighteen, with my first ever curfew.

The breaking point came that summer. I'd wanted to be normal so badly, but normal was no longer on the map. My grandma had just been diagnosed with terminal cancer. I had lost my friends, I had lost my parents' trust—all in the quest for something I was learning didn't exist. (And if it did, I couldn't have it.) I sat with my friend Mike one night, breaking beer bottles against the asphalt road and letting it all go. It started to rain and I made my choice.

"This one is for the farce that is love," I yelled, breaking a bottle against the ground, sparks flying up in the dark. It was finally over.

For weeks afterwards, Jason would call my house and I'd let the phone ring, and he'd call again. I got a new phone number. He kept showing up in the middle of the night. I closed my blinds and locked the doors.

He slit his wrists two months later. It turns out that my previous life, the life I had before, *was* totally normal, because it was happening all over again. Fact: people try to kill themselves. They cut themselves to feel again. They forget about their friends. They place blame when they can't make sense of things. They taunt and they tease and then they apologize. And somewhere in between, you find the time to make out under the stairs and go to school dances. And *that's* totally normal.

The hospital called me one morning in August. He had been discharged. "Your boyfriend left some letters here for you," the nurse told me. My stomach was in my throat. But for the first time in months, the words came easily: "He's not my boyfriend."

Tethered

Cora Goss-Grubbs

When Julie called me that Saturday morning, I was probably sulking in my room, trying to write in my first real journal. I could have been rifling through the box of memories I'd begun, the one with my brother's Sex Pistols cassettes and punk poems, the bars of Sex Wax that he used on his surfboard, and the newspaper articles about his death and funeral. In one of those articles, there was a photo of a young punk placing a red rose on Michael's casket, me in the background looking small and sad, awkward in my thirteen-year-old body and a dress I didn't want to wear.

I picked up the phone on the first ring.

"Cora," Julie said. "My dad killed himself."

I laughed. I actually laughed. Because it was impossible that her father would die just three weeks after my brother was killed in a fight at a party.

"Cora. Stop. He's dead."

I did stop. The pain in her voice finally reached me, deep inside where my own anguish was just starting to crack through the numbness.

"Oh my god. Julie."

We'd known each other for three years, but that's the moment our real friendship began: Julie and I in our separate homes, tethered by a phone line that stretched across town. It transmitted the deepest pain we would ever feel, and it bound us to each other. Twenty-five years later, that connection is still real.

For the next two years, Julie and I were inseparable. Our grieving swerved from serious to silly, sometimes within minutes. We made friends easily with others who had experienced tragedy, and those who shared our fascination with death. We played with Ouija boards at slumber parties until we were too chilled to continue. We snuck out of our houses in the middle of the night and walked two miles on a busy road to the cemetery. We'd sit on my brother's gravestone, smoke clove cigarettes, and talk about why this happened to us. It made us different, special, even invincible. We reasoned that we'd already experienced the worst that can happen—a death in the family. Surely we were safe from any more harm.

There was no memorial marker for Julie's father. His ashes had been spread over the ocean. With him in the sea, and Mike's love of surfing, the California beaches also became a place of solace. Saturday mornings we'd take the bus from Saratoga to Santa Cruz, an hour's ride, and spend the day on the beach. Boys were intrigued by us, our unusually close connection, our sadness. Sometimes I used it to my advantage. "My brother died in a fight at a party," I'd say quietly, at the right moment. Sometimes a boy had even heard of it, in the newspaper or at school. He'd feel sorry for me, put his arm around me, hold me close. But the moment would often turn awkward and fake, and I'd find my way back to Julie, where I felt safe and totally, completely, understood.

Slowly—so slowly—Julie and I veered onto our own grieving paths. Julie struggled with the fear that she might succumb to the same mental illness as her father, and the guilt of a parent's suicide. I was haunted by the private life my brother never shared with his family. I searched for a way into the side of Mike I never knew.

Then I met Marshall through Devin, Mike's best friend. They played in a band together that Devin started after Mike died. An attractive, shy, and moody musician, Marshall drew me into my brother's circle of friends. I hoped they would share with me the secrets they'd shared with him. I believed that life was trying to make up for itself, that an unusual amount of luck was being heaped on me to make up for my giant loss.

Marshall and his bandmates were as inseparable as Julie and I had once been. I felt like an outsider in the punk scene; nonetheless, I inserted myself into their lives and got lost in the smoke and music and Marshall's eyes. Lost in this idea that as long as I was with them, I was with my brother, too. While they played music and partied, I pieced together that other side of Mike. He wrote poetry and lyrics despite his learning disabilities, he was fiercely loyal and hung out with everybody: punkers, surfers, stoners, poets, musicians, nerds.

The more I knew, the more I felt transformed from his annoying little sister to an acquaintance, a comrade even.

For a while, this bond distracted me from the dysfunction of the band members and their friends. They hid from their own messy lives in the basement where they practised, drank cheap beer, and watched hours of TV. They teased me the way my brother had; to them I was still Mike's little sister. I tried to draw Marshall away, but Devin clung to him; he wasn't about to lose another best friend. Gradually, Devin shared less of my brother with me, and less of Marshall with me, too. After six months, I broke up with Marshall, hoping he'd come running back to me. He didn't.

In my grief, I sought out Julie. But she had fallen too far into her own despair to help me. I sank into a sadness that hurt as much as the day I held my brother's hand and watched his braindead body get unplugged from a life support system and die. I no longer had my brother, my blood sister, or my lover. I was totally, utterly alone.

I found salvation in writing. If my brother could do it, so could I. I wrote feverishly, in my journal and for school. I joined the school newspaper, stayed up late with my co-editors, creating words and images from nothing. The act of creation kept me going, kept me grounded. I watched as Julie drifted farther and farther away.

One night, I got a phone call from Julie's mom.

"Have you seen Julie?" she asked.

Julie's phone call three years earlier came rushing back to me. "No," I replied.

"She left a note that says she ran away from home. You haven't heard from her?" Her voice quivered with fear.

"No. I'm sorry. I'll let you know if I do."

After hanging up, I thought about calling Marshall. I knew he would come to me. He would hold me as long as I needed. And, eventually, he would leave. And I would be alone again.

Instead, I went out to my backyard. It was warm and clear, and the new moon was a small tear in the vast blanket of stars above me. I lay on the grass and stared at every part of that great big sky until it made me dizzy.

"Julie?" I asked the night, feeling silly. "Are you okay?"

I needed to know she was alive. I needed to know, selfishly, that she still loved me. Julie had become a part of me, a spare heart when my own had been broken. And now that spare was aching, too. I needed to know it could be fixed.

In that moment, lying flat on my back and feeling myself spinning in the vast universe, I felt again the lifeline that tethered Julie and me to each other. I realized then that it was strong and pliable, that it could survive this brief strain as she drifted off to find herself. I just needed to hold on, to be here when she returned.

And she did.

This is Not From a Place of Perfect Memory

Sarah Pinder

We would play Barbies in your bedroom with the door shut, under the guise of getting away from your younger brother and sister, but really I wanted your body pressed into mine, the thick width of your waist in my hands feeling forbidden back when I was more bones and knees and long, long hair than anything else. We would lie on the bed you shared with your younger sister, the acrylic blanket mashed between our thighs. I imagine that you kissed me, but I think our faces thrust past each other's lips and into the mattress, up to the ceiling, mouthing the names of places we hadn't really been yet.

Easter Seals paid for you to take a trip to Toronto, and you came back with post cards of Casa Loma. I tried to understand a castle in the middle of the city. It looked over-wrought in the souvenir book you'd gotten, and I found myself thinking of my father, renovating the house he just bought, gutting all the smoked mirrors and the gilded wallpaper from the place and hauling them to the dump. I began to think of Toronto as that place of honeyed light, of shag rugs and tasseled lamps, and I wasn't sure if I really wanted to go there, but I envied the independence you'd been given.

Your house had cracked linoleum and in the basement a beer fridge with a Pink Floyd sticker on the door, surrounded by boxes and boxes of empties. My father drank more secretly, liquor that you'd pour into glasses and mix with water and ice. Our parents had grown up in the same neighborhood, but we never talked about how much they had in common. Your mother had that red in her eye sometimes, the blood vessels burst and supernova-ed. The mine was just beginning to close, and your father was home more and angry more, but you never told me that you were afraid. And that smell, the lingering yeast of booze and home-rolled smokes, I knew it well enough to not think twice.

And oh, my girl, we'd sit on your front porch on that broken street together in the thick of late spring afternoons, after school, eating corrugated wafer cookies until our mouths abraded, swearing and singing.

The girls at school would trash-talk your high-waisted jeans and arthritic hands in the locker room after gym class. They'd get me too—my horse teeth, my mother dating the geography teacher—whatever they thought they could grab. I was afraid they'd know we were friends, but I was even more afraid they would know that we'd touched each other, been lovers. I don't remember the day I sold you out, but I know I did it, slouching away from you at my locker and speed-walking out the double doors to stack my odds of popularity.

It never worked, and the thing was, even when I'd figured out that it didn't work, I still held fast to avoiding you. I wrote furiously, cooked up zines late Friday nights when I knew we were both home alone, while all those pretty, straight-toothed girls were out drinking in the bush and fucking their boyfriends in tents. I met a boy from out of town and began to get on the Greyhound and leave, couch-surfing Sudbury basements for weeks, getting kicked out of the bars he was playing in, and walking everywhere, combing new downtown cores where no one knew me, too broke to do much beyond buy a bus ticket to get to them. I saw you around sometimes and you always said hello, had found a man from out of town who you were talking about moving in with. He was older, rail thin, with a sheaf of poker straight hair and a flat, pale name, and you were smitten. I was satisfied—you were happy, I was happy, and we'd both proved those girls wrong.

I moved to Toronto, and found myself missing all the thick weather systems of home. I missed the fat ravens hopping across the highway leading out of town. And I missed you. Home at Christmas, I walked past your house, the driveway piled high with snow, unploughed since the beginning of winter. I was told your family had all left town, in different directions, but I saw your mother one afternoon while walking home. She had a fat lip and a pizza box, the same supernova in her right eye, and she said my name, but she had that sweet smell and sway and couldn't tell me about you. I didn't know what to say. The street lamps were just flickering on, and we stood there on the sidewalk, looking at each other.

She died that spring, when I was back in the city. My mother told me about the funeral, seeming surprised when I went silent.

I asked about you.
I asked about you.
No one could tell me about you.

Emma Please

Tara-Michelle Ziniuk

Her name used to be Emma-Leigh. Emma-Leigh and a last name. But when I met her, she was Emma Please.

I asked her for a cigarette, back when there was smoking in bars, bars that neither of us would admit to going to. We let people assume we met another way: a demo, a meeting, an obvious connection. It wasn't true. She gave me the cigarette, stared, and said, "You don't smoke, do you?"

This interaction repeated the next time we met, over raspberry wheat beer or something else that disappears when you stop living in a college town. "You don't drink beer, do you?" I didn't. She whispered to her roommate at the bar, muted negotiations and pointed looks in my direction. Her roommate didn't come home that night.

Around the one-bedroom apartment limped the Cone Cat, which Emma Please had rescued the weekend before. The cat-in-the-cone didn't look impressed. I was. Her apartment was littered with benefit CDs, flyers from events I'd never heard of, pamphlets on imprisoned radicals, posters of girls who looked like her, with her shaved head and symmetrical piercings.

Emma let me love her with this love that was more than infatuation: it was like illuminated rage. She was insistent on immediately fierce connections, and I was swept into her whirlwind ways. I loved her attention, her world. I believed anything she said when she spoke softly and paused a lot, like she was making claims she'd never made before. I didn't know that I was a secret. I didn't care. Emma Please was a bruised cherry that was still more than I'd ever wanted. To me, she was perfect.

She hated her name—thought it sounded "too *Little House on the Prairie*." She called herself Lee all through high school in a defiance that wasn't about gender so much as typical rebellion against her parents. By the end of high school, she'd gone back to "Emma."

"Please" was added on after the Republican National Convention in Philly. When she and forty others were arrested, she'd called a cop "Sir." Her east-coast American friends decided this act of arbitrary politeness was a Canadian thing, and renamed her Emma Please. I wrote poetry about it: heard it breathed desperate and sexual. Pretended she was named after Emma Goldman. I imagined her mother chastising a tiny rebel with her fingers in the batter, "Emma, *please*."

My First Revolutionary Love brought me to talks where men with forgettable names talked about wars I had no context for. She crawled into my bed after protests, her coat and neck caked in raw egg from friendly fire, and I filled afternoons adoring her. We sewed matching patches on to our pants and backpacks with dental floss. She brought me to marches without police escorts, red and black lines drawn diagonally across flags. Taught me about letting your body go limp when being dragged by cops. Marched me to police headquarters mid-May in Montreal; took photos of the bruises they gave her for all the local papers. I'd heard friends compare boyfriends to drugs, but Emma wasn't what I was addicted to. I wanted to be part of her world.

She encouraged me to read her diary and gave me all of her passwords one of the first times we met. I read about her sexual past and family, her flight from the hometown of golf courses and optometrists' offices— things we otherwise never spoke about. I read about confronting skinheads, toxic shock syndrome, political prisoners, and anti-choice groups. I read while she worked a part-time library job. There was a lot of time to read, and since I had no income, there wasn't much else to do.

With Emma, suddenly there were nights spent drinking in Chinatown after meetings and communal dinners in an apartment in Little Italy, secured before rents skyrocketed. She brewed her own beer and kept huge vats of red wine stored on high kitchen shelves. She grew herbs in windowsill planters; made flowers into medicine, and managed to make it all look hardcore.

I watched her glow in the spotlight. She made me feel bigger than anything I'd known, all chanted slogans were true and anything was possible. She was duct tape and combat boots. She made everything better. I was so distracted by her life that I forgot about mine. I was quiet a lot while

I was with Emma Please, almost silent.

I knew how it would end from the beginning, our romance. Emma was leaving "maybe forever" a few months after we met. This was always part of the draw. We fell in love fast, and I forgot everything I knew before her. In the movie version, I would chase after her, but in reality I tried to look for work and fall back into my pre-Emma existence.

She called once, a couple of days after leaving. "I wish I could have taken you with me," she said quietly into the phone. I needed to believe her.

She came back from time to time, sometimes without my knowing. Once we met in a chic establishment for Americanos. Her mother had washed the wood smoke out of her sweatshirt, but she was still dirtier than I'd ever seen her, with matted hair and an infected bridge piercing. She told stories of riot cop invasions and summit hopping, named girls she'd met sleeping in cavernous stadiums in Prague after the action had ended and the activists were left displaced. Her traveling partner had given birth and flown home, she told me, and named her white daughter after a city in Iraq because she was born on the first day of US bombings.

She took off again to work on an uncle's house, then continued on to "save an old growth forest or herself," whichever came first, she told me.

This time, I wasn't waiting for her to tell me she wanted me to come with her. I didn't want to go.

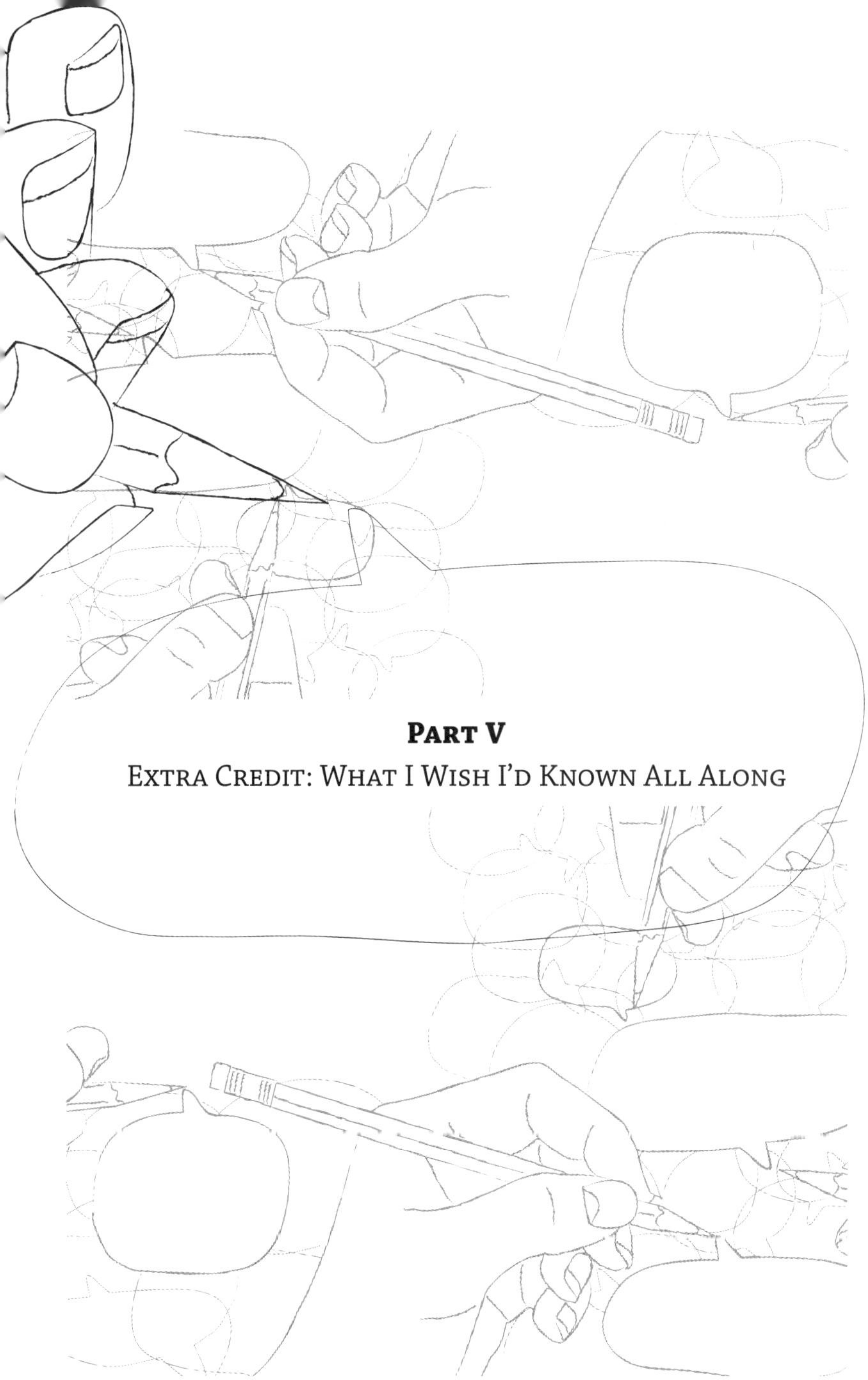

Part V

Extra Credit: What I Wish I'd Known All Along

What I Learned Growing Up In Parkdale

Emily Pohl-Weary

For S.B.

Cars never stop for pedestrians
Kids should buy cigarettes in ones, it's cheaper
Lake Ontario was once clean enough to swim in
Cadillacs invariably carry pimps
You can't find parking on Sundays
Never trust others
Pick your nose when a pusher approaches
If you steal, you'll get beat to a pulp
The cops only make you bleed worse
Guardian Angels are worse than cops
Hookers earn a decent living
The pimp always gets tired
Old women live alone
Boys trick you into giving them blow jobs
Residents' associations hassle single women
The guy who owns the grocery store kicks his workers
My babysitter turns tricks
After dark, every car carries one man
Hide-and-seek is a dangerous game
People can survive anything

THINGS I WISH SOMEONE HAD TOLD ME AS A TEENAGED GIRL

Written by Zoe Whittall, illustrated by Suzy Malik

10. You don't have to be the bass player or the singer.
(This was the era of grunge rock, so perhaps the bass player thing no longer applies.)
Regardless, you can be the songwriter, the drummer, the whatever you want to be in a band-like scenario, without simply being the girl accessory.

9. You have the right to make choices about your body and it's no one else's business but yours.

It's totally okay if you don't want to have sex. It's totally okay if you do want to have sex.

No one is better for choosing either option. Read about it, experiment, figure out what you like for yourself.

This will be helpful in getting over annoying hang-ups.

8. Don't sleep with a boy who doesn't know the exact location of the clitoris or asks for head without returning the favour.
map of the female body

7. If you really hate your high school, leave. Find an alternative school. There's no reason you have to sit at the lunch table next to morons who want you to feel like a waste of skin. If you can make active choices about how and what you're learning, you'll likely be more engaged.

6. If your boyfriend or girlfriend is 25 and you are 16, chances are they are a bit socially inept.
You can't see this now and that's okay, just know you're likely a bit smarter than they are.
They might still be a totally awesome, sweet person, but know that after graduation, you're going to want to check out your other options.

5. Sluts don't exist.

It's a misogynistic double-standard, pure and simple.

People who like sex and can talk about it and make choices they want to make, are evolved, rare, awesome people, no matter the gender.

4. If you want to be a writer, you first have to be a reader.
Stray from your English class reading list.
You don't have to like Catcher in the Rye.

3. Your poetry is probably awful but keep writing it.
Don't show anyone until you've written a third draft.
Eliminate the generalities. Avoid the words: soul, rose, darkness, love, falling, rain, heart. Write about specifics. Your life is interesting enough to write about, in all its gory details.

2. That tattoo is a bad idea,
but may make a funny, nostalgic
story later, before you
cover it up.
Sam

1. Adults are just as clueless as everyone else in the world. Once you become one, you won't suddenly know everything about everything.

If you have been blessed with semi-okay, even slightly awesome parents, like I was, you probably still think they're annoying/controlling/evil right now. If you often feel like you have no idea what you're doing, the feeling is probably mutual.

Cut them a break every once in a while.

Your Mother Was The Wild One

Lynn Bartels

So you pierced your lower lip. Frankly, it looks better than the purple streaks in your hair. Somehow bright colours never show well on brunettes.

But your mother, my sister, is in a state of apoplexy over this new development, so I have come for dinner. With every onion she slices, her frustration wafts into the air. You pretend not to notice, and I just sit and smile.

Aunts get to do that.

See, your mother was the wild one. She snuck out at night, drank herself silly, and gave blow jobs in the dark. She smoked cigarettes in the backyard and borrowed my ID.

Oh—did I say borrowed? Actually, she went to the License Bureau with my social security card and had my driver's license reissued with her picture on it. You could do that then, before computers.

She skipped high school classes in Columbus and went to lunch with her friends in Cincinnati. She forged my father's signature so often that the one time he sent in a real note they would not accept it. Consequently she served a detention for missing a day she really didn't skip.

She drove a mile with a flat tire instead of calling for help, just so our parents wouldn't find the six-pack of beer she had in the back seat or the pot she had in the glove compartment. I lent her money to repair our mother's car when she dented the door. I lent her money for the ticket she got for speeding. More than a few nights I held her hair while she threw up.

And on one autumn Saturday I sat with her before her abortion while she cried.

After all the nights and fights and fretting, she turned out to be—well, your mother. No prison, no addiction, no homelessness. From what I can tell, her rebellion against the staid expectations of society led her to be a politically active adult, an earth-conscious liberal, and an involved, loving parent.

And now as I listen to the two of you argue I'm surprised to hear echoes of our mother in my sister's words.

When she turns and asks me what I think, I know I should back her up with statements of concern. But I doubt I'll sound convincing. The actions of defiance you take to find your independence don't worry me. I am relaxed because I already know the end of this story. I have watched it all before.

You see—your mother was the wild one.

About The Contributors:

K. Bannerman's work has appeared in such journals as *Parabola, Lichen, Herizons,* and *Room Of One's Own,* and in anthologies from Omnidawn Press and St. Martin's Press. She currently lives in a very small house, with her husband, her daughter, and very large dog named Loki, and is working on her third novel. Visit her website at www.kbannerman.com.

Lynn Bartels lives in Ohio with her two college-age sons, one cat, and one dog. Fortunate enough to be able to semi-retire in her forties, she works as a substitute teacher when the mood strikes. Part of the distinguished Nakedwordshop Writer's group, her current credits include essays in *Just Like a Girl: A Manifesto, Mothers and Sons,* and *Anthology* and *Serendipity* magazines. She is honoured to have secured representation by Nancy Coffey for her first fiction novel.

Jowita Bydlowska was born in Warsaw but now lives and likes it in Toronto.

Maggie Dort is 1/3 blood and 2/3 guts.

Nicole Cohen is the co-founder of *Shameless* and co-edited the magazine's first nine issues. She is currently a PhD candidate in the graduate program in Communication and Culture at York University. Nicole has written for a variety of independent and alternative Canadian magazines, and her academic work has been published in *Democratic Communiqué Stream,* and *Feminist Media Studies.* She is involved in several media-related projects, including Media Action and *Upping The Anti: A Theory of Journal and Action.*

Shannon Gerard makes things with her hands—she writes and draws sappy autobiographical comics, spends 50% of her waking life crocheting soft sculptures, binds books, and makes screenprints. Two current projects are the illustrated serial *Unspent Love (or Things I Wish I Told You)* for Top Shelf Productions and the post-apocalyptic graphic novel *Sword of My Mouth* with writer Jim Munroe. Shannon's nickname at summer camp was "The Plains of Abraham"—a hilarious reversal of the popular Christian camp ditty "Rock my Soul in the Bosom of Abraham." More of Shannon's stuff can be found at www.shannongerard.org.

Cora Goss-Grubbs lives in Woodinville, Washington, with her spouse and two sons, in a home sandwiched between a blueberry farm and a wetland. Her essays, poems, and interviews have been published in *Pontoon 10* (an anthology of Washington state poets), *Between the Lines*, *Calyx*, *StringTown*, *hipMama*, *Synapse*, *Victory Review,* and aired on public radio. She is a 1998 Hedgebrook alumna and 2003 Jack Straw Productions writer-in-residence. Cora founded RASP, a non-profit organization that hosts literary events for adults, teens, and children, and seeks a publisher for her two young adult novels.

Catherine Graham is the author of *The Watch*, *Pupa*, and *The Red Element*. She teaches creative writing at the University of Toronto, the Haliburton School of the Arts, and through the City of Burlington. Her work has been anthologized internationally and published in *The New Quarterly*, *Literary Review of Canada*, *Taddle Creek*, and *The Fiddlehead*. She is Vice President of Project Bookmark Canada and Marketing Coordinator for the Rowers Pub Reading Series. www.catherinegraham.com

Jessica Lockhart is a Ryerson University journalism graduate and a former editor of *McClung's Magazine: Ryerson's Voice for Women*. She lives in Toronto, plays too much Scrabble, and doesn't miss northern Albertan winters.

E. J. MacBain is a writer and editor living in the Northeast. Her nonfiction has previously appeared in *hipMama* magazine. She is the proud feminist mama of a toddler son and a baby daughter.

Suzy Malik is motivated by the powerful pairings of pictures and words. She has a BFA in New Media (which can likely explain her love of *MIT* magazine). She happily calls Toronto home. Her day job involves art directing handsome boys and helping to come up with cheeky marketing campaigns. She spends some of her free time designing, writing, and illustrating.

In her *actual* free time she makes art in all kinds of mediums and reads all things graphic novel-y.

Melinda Mattos is the co-founder of *Shameless*, and co-edited the magazine's first nine issues. Since obtaining her bachelor of journalism in 2003, she's taken a whirlwind tour of the industry, working at the *Toronto Star*, *The Globe and Mail*, TVOntario, Magazines Canada, and *EYE WEEKLY*. On the rare occasions she's not working, Melinda enjoys yelling into microphones and playing bass with her punk band, The Weirdies.

Jessica McGann is obsessed with her cat and her vagina, but swears she leads a rich and full life.

Adrienne Mercer lives in Nanaimo, B C. She has published creative non-fiction in *Lost* magazine and the 2007 Anvil Press anthology *Body Breakdowns*, and is also the author of a young adult novel called *Rebound* (Lorimer Canada, 2002). She and her husband Michael recently had their first child—a son.

Nicole Pasulka is a writer and editor. You can visit her at www.missthunderstood.com, or in Brooklyn, NY, where she lives with a very funny-looking dog.

Pam Park Jost is a bona fide product of the '80's, and is the drummer for indie pop/rock bands who create songs about love and heartache. When she's not playing, she spends her time in an office as an Employment Counsellor at the Multilingual Orientation Service Association for Immigrant Communities. Currently residing in Vancouver, BC, Pam has been lucky enough to spend her 20's and most of her 30's living, working, and playing in New York City, San Francisco, and Seoul.

Tara-Michelle Ziniuk is an author, activist, performer, and media maker. She likes indie young adult fiction and lives between Guelph and Toronto with a hedgehog named Francine. Check out her latest book of poetry, *Somewhere To Run From*. Her blog can be found at therealtmz.blogspot.com.

Sarah Pinder grew up in Northern Ontario and presently calls Toronto home. A zine-maker of nearly ten years, her work has been shortlisted for the Expozine Small Press Awards, as well as published in *undercurrents* and *Canadian Woman Studies*.

Emily Pohl-Weary is the author of five books (including the novel *A Girl Like Sugar* and the poetry collection *Iron-on Constellations*) and the editor of an anthology about female superheroes (*Girls Who Bite Back*). She also runs the Parkdale Street Writers, a free writing workshop for youth in west-end Toronto. Visit her at www.emilypohlweary.com.

Denise Reich was born in Italy and grew up in New York and Maine. She moved more than fourteen times and went to ten different schools before she was sixteen, so she's not really sure where she is from. Her work has appeared in various publications in the USA, Bermuda, South Africa, and elsewhere, and has tackled issues ranging from the Chernobyl disaster to Beanie Babies. She was the co-author, illustrator, and editor of *We're In Print!*, a guide for young journalists sponsored by UNICEF and Young Voices/Norway and currently listed as a resource by UNICEF's Child and Youth Participation Guide.

Amy Saxon Bosworth lives and writes from her home in the mountains outside of Nederland, Colorado. Her essays have been featured in *Hearing Loss Magazine*, *Mamaphonic,* and *Hands and Voices*. Her novella *The Mean Time* was a 2006 semi-finalist for Tin House's Summer Literary Seminar, Kenya. Her writing was also included in the anthology *My Baby Rides the Short Bus* (PM Press, 2009). She is currently at work on her second novel.

Julia Serano is a writer, spoken word artist, trans activist, and biologist based in Oakland, California. She is the author of *Whipping Girl: A Transsexual Woman on Sexism and the Scapegoating of Femininity* (Seal Press, 2007), a collection of personal essays that reveal how misogyny frames popular assumptions about femininity and shapes many of the myths and misconceptions people have about transsexual women. Julia's other writings have appeared in anthologies (including *BITCHfest: Ten Years of Cultural Criticism from the Pages of* Bitch *Magazine,* and *Word Warriors: 30 Leaders in* *the Women's Spoken Word Movement*), in feminist, pop culture, and literary magazines (such as *Bitch, Clamor, Kitchen Sink, make/shift, other, LiP,* and *Transgender Tapestry*), and have been used as teaching materials in college-level gender studies courses across the United States. For more information, check out www.juliaserano.com.

Dianah Smith is a Jamaican-born, Ottawa-raised writer, teacher, curator, and arts educator based in Toronto. She is the Founder of A is for Orange, a reading series featuring queer Caribbean emerging writers (www.aisfororange.org). Dianah is the recipient of several grants including an emerging writer's grant from the Toronto Arts Council and a Writing Mentorship grant from the Ontario Arts Council. She enjoys facilitating autobiographical writing workshops in schools and with community groups in the city. She says, "Writing is a way to grieve/retrieve the past, make sense of the present and leave a legacy for the future."

Shaunga Tagore is a self-proclaimed singer-songstress, warrior-poet, gangsta-feminist, extreme-ranter-queen, lover-fighter, soul-sista-diva, who dreams of a world without hierarchies and categories, and watches *Buffy* in her spare time.

Teri Vlassopoulos wrote the zines *Melt the Snow* between 1997 and 2002 and *The Second Part* between 2002 and 2004. Her latest zine, *Cement, Flour, Saints*, was released in November 2007. She is currently working on a novel.

Dr. Karma Waltonen is a lecturer in the writing program at the University of California, Davis. Former president of the Margaret Atwood Society, she facilitates weekly meetings of the Margaret Atwood Book Club of Davis (though the name is somewhat misleading as they ran out of Atwood texts to read years ago). She is a writer, comedian, and Simpsonologist (and has a forthcoming book on teaching *The Simpsons*). You can find her blog at www.dr-karma.com.

Shannon Webb-Campbell tends to leave belletristic impressions, as she waxes poetic about music, literature, and art to everyone she meets. As a lifelong student, she holds a degree in journalism and English literature from Dalhousie University and Durham College. Her writing and photography can be found in *Room*, *Chart*, *The Coast*, *Xtra!*, *Penguin Eggs*, *Bitch*, and *Broken Pencil*. If you ask her where she's from she'll tell you she's a Newfoundlander, even though she was raised in Ontario, born in Alberta, and now lives in Halifax, NS.

Zoe Whittall is the author of the novel *Bottle Rocket Hearts* and three books of poetry, most recently *Precordial Thump*. Her second novel is forthcoming in the fall of 2009 with House of Anansi Press.

Acknowledgments

Shameless would like to thank all of our fabulous and feisty contributors, staff, and volunteers who, over the past five years, have made the mag the vital resource for teenage girls it is today. We would also like to thank our readers, subscribers, and supporters, without whom none of this would have been possible.

Stacey May would like to thank Halli Villegas and the fine folks at Tightrope Books for saying yes to and supporting this project without hesitation. Thanks to the inspiring staff at *Shameless* magazine, most of all Megan Griffith-Greene, who knows the value of a steak and martini dinner, always greets you with a hug, and makes absolutely everything happen with unbelievable humility. Thanks to my mom and dad for trusting and supporting my ever-evolving passions, as strange as they always seemed. Thanks to Conan Tobias for helping me fully realize why, and how much, I truly love magazines. Gratitude goes to the Toronto small magazine and literary communities for good advice, conversation, and, occasionally, a debauched night on the town. Finally, endless love and thanks to Spencer, who has been a sounding board and a pillar from the start.

Megan has so much love for Stacey May for making this all happen, and for being the most brilliant, inspiring, shameless partner in crime a girl could hope for. Thanks to the staff of *Shameless*, especially our lovely and talented art director Sheila, and to Nicole and Melinda for their wisdom and for trusting me with their baby. Thanks also to the staff of *Chatelaine* for giving me the freedom to follow the curious tendrils of my career. Thanks to my kickass friends and family, especially my mum, Honor Griffith, for unending support and for instilling the seeds of civil disobedience even before I learned the alphabet. And my love and gratitude to Jeromy Lloyd, for patience and calm in the chaos, and for all the backrubs.

About The Editors:

Stacey May Fowles' writing has appeared in various online and print magazines, including *Kiss Machine*, *Broken Pencil*, *Fireweed*, and *subTERRAIN*. Her work has been widely anthologized in books, including *Nobody Passes: Rejecting The Rules of Gender and Conformity*, *First Person Queer*, *Yes Means Yes*, and *I.V. Lounge Nights*. Her first novel, *Be Good*, was published by Tightrope Books in 2007, and *This Magazine* called it "probably the most finely realized small press novel to come out of Canada in the last year." Fowles recently adapted her second novel, *Fear of Fighting*, into a stage play as part of Nightwood Theatre's Write From The Hip program for emerging female playwrights. She currently lives in Toronto where she is the publisher of *Shameless* magazine. www.staceymayfowles.com

Megan Griffith-Greene's experience in activism, arts, and journalism started when she was a very shameless teen in Toronto. She is the editor of *Shameless* magazine, and a researcher at *Chatelaine*. She is also a founding editor and designer of *The New Pollution* new music review, and a past editor of the *Ryerson Review of Journalism*. Her writing has appeared in *This Magazine*, *The Walrus*, and *Chatelaine*.

ABOUT SHAMELESS MAGAZINE:

Founded in June 2004, *Shameless* is Canada's independent voice for smart, strong, sassy young women. It's a fresh alternative to typical teen magazines, for girls who know there's more to life than makeup and diet tips. Packed with articles about arts, culture, and current events, *Shameless* reaches out to readers who are often ignored by mainstream media: freethinkers, queer youth, young women of colour, punk rockers, feminists, intellectuals, artists, activists—people just like you! We tackle teen life with wit and wisdom.

Proudly independent, *Shameless* is a grassroots magazine produced by a team of volunteer staff members, with content guided by a teen advisory board.

Each issue of *Shameless* entertains and inspires with profiles of amazing women, discussion of the hot topics that concern you most, DIY guides to crafty activities, sports dispatches, the latest in technology, columns on food politics, health and sexuality, advice, and more.

Subscribe at www.shamelessmag.com/subscribe